Saving Arabella

A Memoir:
A Domestic Violence Asylum Seeker Story

BRENDA PETERSEN

First published by Ultimate World Publishing 2024
Copyright © 2024 Brenda Petersen

ISBN

Paperback: 978-1-923123-44-1
Ebook: 978-1-923123-45-8

Brenda Petersen has asserted her rights under the Copyright, Designs and Patents Act 1988 to be identified as the author of this work. The information in this book is based on the author's experiences and opinions. The publisher specifically disclaims responsibility for any adverse consequences which may result from use of the information contained herein. Permission to use information has been sought by the author. Any breaches will be rectified in further editions of the book.

All rights reserved. No part of this publication may be reproduced, stored in or introduced into a retrieval system, or transmitted in any form, or by any means (electronic, mechanical, photocopying, recording or otherwise) without the prior written permission of the author. Any person who does any unauthorised act in relation to this publication may be liable to criminal prosecution and civil claims for damages. Enquiries should be made through the publisher.

Cover design: Ultimate World Publishing
Layout and typesetting: Ultimate World Publishing

Ultimate World Publishing
Diamond Creek,
Victoria Australia 3089
www.writeabook.com.au

*"You're beautiful, but no one loves you;
no one likes to marry you!"
– ex-husband*

I acknowledge and show respect to the First Nations, Traditional Owners and the continuing connection of Aboriginal and Torres Strait Islander peoples to the Country

Disclaimer

This memoir is a truthful recollection of actual events in the author's life. Some events have been compressed and some dialogues have been recreated. To respect their privacy, the names and details of some individuals have been changed.

Note from Author

This book contains physical, emotional, mental, verbal and sexual abuse, suicidal thoughts, suicidal attempts stories and mental illness that may be a trigger to some readers.

In telling my story the feelings, emotions, thoughts and memories are their own, and they deserve the respect I give by only writing about my perspectives.

I advocate for mental health well-being. Although I am not a psychologist, I studied more than 40 units of family psychology, family counselling and theories of personality, and I am a proud teacher who became passionate about writing after I left my abusive marriage. I also wish to impart my advocacy of domestic violence intergenerational trauma patterns of abuse of control and mental well-being through this book.

Please call your GP SUPPORT LINES:
National: 1800 RESPECT, 1800 737 732
MensLine Australia: 1300 789 978
Kids Helpline: 1800 55 1800

Lifeline 131114 for anyone who may be needing help after reading my book. I hope you find inspiration despite the sensitive issues that may trigger your own precious life stories. Enjoy the journey of reading my book.

SAVING ARABELLA

To my mother, Corazon, who fought the good fight in life and loved too much to a fault – I made you proud of your youngest daughter here in Australia!

To Arabella, you are my saving grace to live again and have the courage to rebuild my life with you – I made you proud as my youngest daughter here in Australia!

To my *unico hijo*, only son, Josh Benedict, I made you proud as my only son here in Australia!

To my firstborn child as a teenage mum, I devoted myself to you. At almost 2 years old, you read all the flashcards I gave to you, and you memorised a ladybird Cinderella book on your 6th birthday. I am proud of you that you were like Mum, played Helena in A *Midsummer Night's Dream* school play, and most of all, for being the former Spokesperson for the Vice President of the Philippines a Harvard University Outstanding Graduate. Thanks for all these gifts of achievements you gave to me as your mother.

To all mothers-in-law, I always have care, love and respect for all of you. No matter what happens, I count you in my heart.

Testimonials

"A touching story of resilience from a strong woman"
**– Wollondilly Member of Parliament
Judy Hannan**

"I recently had the privilege of reading Bren Petersen's powerful and deeply moving book on domestic violence, and I cannot emphasize enough the impact it had on me. Bren's journey from victim to survivor is not just a story; it's a testament to the strength of the human spirit and a source of inspiration for every woman.

In her candid narrative, Bren sheds light on the insidious nature of domestic violence, recounting the gradual erosion of her self-esteem and self-worth at the hands of her husband and mother-in-law. She bravely confronts the harsh realities of verbal, mental, and physical abuse, providing a raw and honest account of her experiences that resonates deeply.

What sets Bren's book apart is her openness about the reasons she stayed in the abusive marriage, detailing the isolation from her own family and the suffocating control that bound her. Her escape to Australia marked a pivotal moment in her life, but the effects of intergenerational trauma and abuse lingered, leaving her vulnerable to a new cycle of victimization.

Through the lens of hindsight, Bren reflects on the shadows of those years of abuse and the toll it took on her self-esteem. Yet, in the midst of the darkness, she illuminates the kindness of charities and the crucial support that helped her break free once and for all. Her resilience shines through as she grapples with the ongoing struggle to reclaim her hard-earned self-esteem.

This book is a must-read for anyone seeking insight into the complexities of domestic violence and the enduring impact it can have on survivors. Petersen's story is not just about overcoming adversity; it's a call to action, urging society to stand against domestic violence and support those who bravely break free from its chains. Every woman should read this book – it's a beacon of hope, strength, and ultimately, triumph."

       - Wollondilly Councilor Suzy Brandstater

"Bren's story shows the immense courage, conviction, and community support needed to leave an abusive relationship for good. Abuse is interwoven into all communities. To end abuse, we all need to learn to recognize how common it is, and how brave survivors like Bren are."

    -Leslie Morgan Steiner, New York Times bestselling author of Crazy Love

TESTIMONIALS

"Dear Bren,

Thank you so much for reading my book, The Mother Wound, and for reaching out. I am sorry you have had those experiences but I am glad my book spoke to you and felt relevant. How wonderful to know that you are writing your own Memoir! I hope it is an empowering and cathartic process for you. Wishing you the absolute best with it!"

– **Amani Haydar, Award Winning Author, The Mother Wound, A Memoir about Gender Based Violence, Lawyer turned Artist**

"A journey that will unfortunately resonate with many. The courage and strength to leave everything behind and start again shows Brenda's determination to make a better life - to fight for her self-worth and a future for her daughter. With such a formidable role-model - Arabella has grown into a strong, intelligent and confident young lady, validation all the sacrifices were worth it for both of them. A compelling read!"

- **Melissa Wheeler**
Douglas Park Wilton NSW Physie Dance Owner
Physie Teacher of Arabella
Principal

"I always knew there was something special about you babe from the moment I met you… congratulations you should be so so proud!"

- **Pam, kind and caring mate of Bren**

About The Author

Bren Petersen is a proud single mother to her 14-year-old daughter, Arabella. Originating from the Philippines, their plea for protection in 2014 led them to become asylum seekers in Australia. Arabella stands as the cornerstone of Bren's life – the reason why they moved and the catalyst for her book, Saving Arabella.

A survivor of intergenerational trauma and domestic abuse, Bren aims to impart awareness on her advocacy for mental health and well-being and prevention of domestic violence issues. A passionate, goal-oriented humanitarian and hard worker, Bren puts emphasis on making the world a better place to live in and spreading kindness.

She finished her master of teaching in Basic Education Teaching K–12 and bachelor of science postgraduate course in Family Counselling and Family Psychology at a private Catholic university in the Philippines, which the NSW Education Standards Authority (NESA) converted to bachelor of teaching Australian curriculum equivalent.

A devoted mother and teacher, she became a Benedictine Oblate with the Missionary Benedictine Sisters of Tutzing Germany in their chapter at St. Scholastica's College, Manila, where she taught for 13 years. She often joined their Lauds (midday prayer) and Vespers (evening prayer).

She loved dancing and was one of the cheer dance teachers during their school's sports day and a volleyball player for 13 years, which was one of the joys she drew from while hiding her abuse. In her spare time, she loves going to the spa and spending time alone, as it nurtured her soul.

After rebuilding her life in Australia, she is currently an esteemed high school teacher in her local Wollondilly community, where she puts focus on her students' mental health and well-being by advocating the use of music and dance for their mental wellness.

Contents

Note from Author	ix
Testimonials	xi
About The Author	xv
Prologue	1
Introduction	5
Hail my mother!	15
I am my mother's daughter: Breaking the intergenerational trauma	21
An Empty Christmas Eve	41
I was supposed to die when I was a baby!	47
Bruce Almighty vs. the Dancing Queen	59
Nightmares, Red Flags & a Car Accident	81
2019 – Rocky, the Unexpected Hero	93
Run to Paradise (Uluru) on my 52nd Birthday	101
Gilee Cried Abuse!	107
An open letter to my dear, beautiful, loving son	125
Begging the God of Australia, hear my plea	131
Epilogue	147
Acknowledgements	161
More Testimonials	165

Prologue

What have I done for nearly 10 years? Still struggling to be protected. Have I been well? Not quite. For nearly 10 years, I have unknowingly been throwing all the toxic psychological, mental, verbal and sexual abuse my ex-husband did to me. What have I been suffering and fearing from? This is my story.

I was tied by unknown people. I looked at them with so much fear, as they electrocuted me on both sides.

I was screaming, but no sound was coming out. Crowds kept asking, "Why are you doing that to her?"

In my mind I questioned, "Why are you all doing this to me?"

I tried to let go, but my hands and whole body are tied. I felt fear in my inner soul.

I opened my eyes and suddenly felt calm. It was just a nightmare!

SAVING ARABELLA

I still remember the date of my nightmare – 15 September 2022. I call it my nightmare saga. I would write the date and the stories of my nightmares in my notes, as it helped me address my mental trauma during counselling.

My mental trauma always comes back to me in my nightmares. I was diagnosed with post-traumatic stress disorder (PTSD) and hypervigilance by the NSW Service for the Treatment and Rehabilitation of Torture and Trauma Survivors (STARTTS), as my fear of returning to a devious, abusive past always haunted me. These fears range from something as simple as being startled to being followed by someone who wants to trouble me.

I befriended my fear. One day at a time, one moment in time. My present moment is safe in spite of the trauma I suffered. I was lucky to befriend my fear through the many true-blue Australians who helped me value and stick up for myself.

The fear of being controlled and manipulated is gone, but the remnants of the trauma left a scar in my DNA. Then, I always think, *I am safe here. My daughter, Arabella, and I are safe here.* One day, my fears will be permanently erased as I gain my permanent freedom.

This is a real-life nightmare I have suffered. This is why I want to share to the world why I have walked away as far as I can and brought Arabella with me. I realised that I was so ready to write this memoir. When my writing coach told me I needed to share the story of how I met my ex-husband, I said no. I didn't want to even remember anything about him. But the magic of healing finally took place! I am now ready to write and connect all the puzzle pieces to form a whole story of how I ended up in this pattern of abuse.

PROLOGUE

Why have I suffered this kind of trauma? Where did this trauma come from? Why did I have to stay long? Why did I stay longer than other women? What have I done to attract all this abuse, trauma and noncommittal men, all while having to be strong in the same breath for my dear Arabella, whom I saved from further manipulation, coercive control, psychological and mental abuse from her father?

My triumphant story catapulted me to model resilience, and there was no other choice for me but to stay strong.

I have been resurrected here in Australia. I always say that this is already my second life. Right now I'm an asylum seeker with my daughter, Arabella, as a result of all this abuse I suffered from my ex-husband.

From riches to rags by choice, I say – I chose to walk away from my ex-husband and his greed for our multi-million peso properties in the Philippines, as he used my adult children to shield all our properties from equal settlement, and gain my freedom to raise Arabella here in Australia.

I wish that women, or even the young adults, who are still stuck in abusive relationships can learn from my book and choose better life decisions. You have a path to walk away from domestic violence. Do not stay too long being abused. Do not ever hide being abused. Spot the red flags early on.

All my stories are my personal insights and my personal life lessons from my years of education learning psychology, counselling, and teaching as well. It may be confronting for some, especially for those who have not experienced domestic violence.

SAVING ARABELLA

Please take note that all the verbal abuse of my ex-husband was said in our native Filipino language, hence they are translated in English with an open closed parenthesis.

I will lead you through the stories about how I saved Arabella and why we have to cut the intergenerational trauma.

Introduction

Why am I writing this book? What have I got to say? Am I that special to think that I can write a memoir? Why did I ever keep this abuse so long? Who am I to share anything special when my ex-husband said, "You are nothing. No one will believe you – not even lawyers or the police will believe you. Even your school employers won't believe you. They only want to talk to me because I have the money!"

This book is not about hatred or maligning anyone involved in the past version of myself. I am writing this book out of empathy. Out of love, not hatred. Out of peace, not anger. Out of joy, not sadness. Out of reconciliation with my inner self-worth. Out of knowledge to break down the intergenerational trauma that I have seen in my family and my family of origin.

This book is meant to share about my innocence and naivety, literally as a minor who entered marriage. I regret getting married early but never regretted having six beautiful children. Why? I never went out or gone dating. I only went out with my then husband.

I am writing this book to show to the world how far I have come. This is to share with the world that we, women, can have a choice to be treated well.

I found an award-winning book entitled See What You Made Me Do by Jess Hill. It is about the phenomenon of domestic abuse and coercive control. It was released in 2019 and awarded the 2020 Stella Prize. In 2021, it was adapted into a series on SBS.

She is a journalist, author and speaker who focuses primarily on social issues and gendered violence. She started her career almost 15 years ago as a producer for ABC Radio, went on to become a Middle East correspondent for The Global Mail, and then an investigative journalist for Background Briefing. Her reporting has won two Walkley awards, an Amnesty International award and three Our Watch awards.

Recent projects include a podcast series on coercive control and patriarchy called The Trap and a quarterly essay on how *#MeToo* has changed Australia, titled The Reckoning. Since the book was released, she has spoken at almost 300 public events about coercive control and regularly conduct training and education for groups as diverse as magistrates, high school students, workplaces and local councils.

This is my plan for this book as well – to advocate and educate high school students, workplaces and the humanity for the awareness of coercive control abuse, which is not necessarily with physical bruise and cuts.

INTRODUCTION

I have researched Kindle books online and found that not many were willing to write about the coercive control and manipulative, mental, psychological, verbal and sexual abuse they have suffered. However, I have seen a memoir on Kindle about controlling and manipulative abuse. It is Adele Bellis's memoir. She also suffered from being controlled and isolated from her family, just like how I suffered.

Whack! A sudden kick landed on my butt. I did not know where it came from, so I looked and saw him, my then-husband Bruce.

"Graduate *ka nga ng* college, *wala namang mangyayari sa'yo.* Bum *ka lang at walang trabaho.*" ("You graduated uni, but nothing will happen to you. You're just a bum. You don't even have work!") Four years into our marriage, Bruce said this to me while I laid down with my sleeping baby in his parents' small wooden room of their heritage house, where we used to stay.

I just graduated at that time. Can I just first find a job?

I said nothing to him.

That was the second physical and verbal abuse I have suffered from him, but I took it aside. The first one was two years into our marriage, when I attended a Rotaract Induction of Officers outside of our school. I came home at 10 pm, which I thought was OK since I attended a school function.

Climbing an old, wobbly wooden stairs of a heritage house was interesting. I must be careful, or I will end up sliding a foot in the space between its steps. But they are the strongest wood, I should say.

As I reached the top of the stairs, the antique wooden door with a vintage brass doorknob slightly opened.

Smack! Bruce punched me on the lip. I cried and said nothing.

His mother saw me crying and saw my lips bleeding. "Do not ever lift your hand to Brenda again", she told her son.

I said nothing to his mother.

I thought that this was just a one-off. In hindsight, he disregarded his mother's reprimand not to physically hurt me. He continued verbally and mentally abusing me and resorted to physical violence – kicking, punching and pinching – to keep me at a distance when we were in bed.

I thought it was my fault. I should have not gone home late. But then again, I did nothing wrong. I attended a school function, as I was part of it. I knew nothing as a 17-year-old wife and mother.

I did not know this was abuse from the start. I did not know anything about a caring, loving relationship. I have not seen one – my mother was a single mother, and I have not seen it from my siblings. One thing that was constant, though, since I was 9 or 10 years old, was my faith in God. I would always quickly eat my Tropical Hut hamburger near my school and run so that I could attend the Holy Mass in my Catholic school; I would read the bible and be a commentator for the daily mass there.

Now, just to say, I do not have "daddy issues", although I had not met my father since he died when I was a baby. With

INTRODUCTION

wisdom now, I say that my father image is God. I have always been spiritual and prayerful. I never faltered in believing in God, and my insurmountable faith led me to where I am now despite what I have gone through.

Unbelievable, isn't it? But it is true. Miracles do happen. I believe that God has made so many miracles in my life and saved me from any danger I know nothing about. That is my faith. Oh, I even got in trouble with my psychology professor in my master's degree in family psychology, taking life transitions. In one of my stories for our assignment, my professor commented, "Brenda, be careful, as you might be over-spiritualising things in your life. Good luck in your journey."

I have never shared with my psychology teacher about all the abuse of my then husband. But in this book, I will say, it was the abuse I was hiding, as my professor thinks there are things I have not unlocked. Truth well be told, I bursted out of all the abuse after 24 years and eight months.

All along, while hiding the abuse, I thought that I would just take it as a challenge and find work. But with my wisdom now as an empowered woman, I'd say that if a man belittles and humiliates you and says you are nothing without him, whether it be a boyfriend or someone you are dating, **run** … as fast as you can.

Don't ever allow any man to belittle you, and you don't have to prove anything to him. He is supposed to be supportive, caring and your cheerleader, not someone who belittles you.

My ex-husband used to hide all our car keys just because I refused to follow his demand to not dance flamenco. He turned off the electricity for that lame reason that I was doing my hobby. Worst of all, not many think this is abuse. They always look at abuse as physical or sexual. But, anything that does not allow you to have your freedom to say and do what you want, including your hobbies or what you wear, is still called abuse. It is called coercive control abuse.

The year was 1995. I was in my early 20s, fresh from university, which Bruce's mother sent me to. I knew nothing about being assertive of my rights then.

"Here is the application form for the tourist visa and the passport", my mother-in-law gave to me.

"Oh, I can just ring the Australian Embassy, as I have my permanent residence. I even told them that I will go next time", I told my mother-in-law and Bruce, engaging in the conversation.

"*Hindi natin kelangan ang* Australia. *Mayaman tayo dito*", my husband told me. ("We don't need Australia. We're rich here.")

I said nothing. Again. My knowledge and understanding of this before were just plain conversations that I had to follow. Yes, my in-laws sent me to school and gave me food and shelter, so I should just follow them and not say how I felt and what I liked in terms of visiting my family in Australia. This was my thought as a 15-year-old wife who lived with her husband's mother.

As I write my story and recall all the abuse I have suffered for 24 years with them, I now know that Bruce and my mother-in-law were controlling me from my rights to gain back my permanent Australian residency. They were isolating me from being with my

INTRODUCTION

own family of origin. They did not want me to ring the Australian Embassy and only allowed me to go if I used a tourist visa so I couldn't permanently stay in Australia.

Now that I have come out of their mother–son tandem of controlling, abusive pattern, I now know that they did not want me to get my permanent residency reinstated to keep me from telling anyone that I was being controlled, isolated and manipulated.

In hindsight, 1995 was the last year I could regain my permanent residency if I had not entered the country for 10 years.

My mother, twin brother and I were sponsored by my elder sister, Maria, for family migration in 1986. I will never forget that moment – I was 15, and I was with my mother in the Australian Embassy. I told the consul that I was staying behind and not going with my mother and twin brother.

"Oh, you are denying our beautiful country", the Consul retorted.

"No," I replied, "I will go later and will get married."

He smiled at me.

Dwelling now into the chapters of my book, my mother knew best, not wanting me to stay back. She wanted me to go and migrate with them in Australia and not marry at 15. She wanted Bruce to follow me to Australia, but my eldest sister opposed.

"Bruce's family has to take care of Brenda and make sure to look after her and send her to school to finish college", she said.

Again, I do not blame anyone – not my mother-in-law, not my eldest sister. They only did what they thought was good and did not know any better. After all, the intergenerational trauma is deep-rooted.

I wonder, what is my ex-husband's childhood trauma that made him abusive instead of the caring, loving and affectionate husband I pictured? Why was my mother overpowered by my eldest sister's decision? And why do I have to walk away as my two oldest daughters disrespected me?

Tying up loose ends here! No blame games.

Love is my greatest shield. I still love my sisters. They were just victims of the past. Healing and coming to terms are the key of this book and why I wrote it. Awareness of breaking the intergenerational trauma in the family is my advocacy here as well.

Right now, I have to beg the current Prime Minister of Australia to give me back my permanent residency.

I am grateful to the Honourable Prime Minister Anthony Albanese, as he always replied when I wrote him emails about my plight for protection and the ongoing abuse to my adult daughter, Gilee, by her father. He referred me to the Honourable Home Affairs Minister to follow up.

I am also grateful to Honourable Judy Hannan, MP for endorsing me to the Honourable Andrew Giles MP, Minister for Immigration, Citizenship and Multicultural Affairs, and I quote, "Please be assured your support has been noted and the information you have provided has been forwarded to the relevant area of

INTRODUCTION

the Department for consideration. Thank you for bringing Ms Hernandez and Miss Arabella's concerns to my attention."

I am indeed lucky to be living in Wollondilly and to have a very supportive true blue local MP, Judy Hannan.

Hail my mother!

When I was in primary school, my mother would wrap tons of Christmas gifts for all the people in the neighbourhood, and she would always drop by my school to give the Christmas gift she had for my classroom teacher. I would kiss my mum goodbye, holding on to the wrapped Christmas gift. As the years went by, I kind of knew it was always a handbag. Thank God I never had a male classroom teacher. But of course, my mum would be ready for it.

Anyway, that was a cute story I remember about my mother – even though we were not that rich, she was generous to the people around her. Now I know why I am generous too. I would buy hundreds of the same Christmas gifts for all my colleagues; say, all 100 umbrellas. I have always been generous and would give a lift to any teacher who needed one. Plus, my house was always open for them to have a snack or dinner, as I live a stone's throw away from the Catholic school where I used to teach in the Philippines. I also would donate if a nun asked for a favour, like when a priest needed a tuition fee.

Like mother, like daughter – generous, kind and loving. I am my mother's daughter, indeed!

One thing I noticed, though, was that she never talked about my father. I never asked when I was younger either, as it felt disrespectful to ask my mother or older siblings about adult topics. That was just how our family dynamic was.

While I was growing up in the Philippines, my mother worked at night, and so when I woke up in the morning, she was sound asleep. I had to be quiet so she won't wake up. On the dining table was a paper that said:

Brenda – *Baon* 75c (school lunch money), Veggie (wet food market) – ₱1

When I went to visit her in Australia at her Airds housing commission in 1995 and 1996, I saw the same thing on her dining table:

Nuggets McDonalds – $2.00; Bus/Train – $2.00

I smiled when I saw it. I did not know why I smiled then. Looking back, my mother was always frugal just to make ends meet as a single mother. She raised her seven kids on her own without a husband.

I look at myself now; since 2011, I have been a single mother. I was like my mother – a frugal single mother who, no matter what happens, would find a way to find a job to make sure that Arabella had food to eat.

HAIL MY MOTHER!

Hail to my mother! She indeed knows best!

If only she had a voice, I would not have been abused for long and isolated in the Philippines. Being isolated from my family in Australia was one thing, but being isolated from my second brother, also residing in the Philippines, was plain despicable. He told me that he once visited me in my in-law's house in Manila. However, my mother-in-law did not treat him nicely, even saying, "Brenda is not here. Don't come here anymore."

I reconnected with my second brother after we had our first dwelling property with Bruce. We lived with my in laws for eleven years . He would come with his two sons and his then partner during Christmas so I could give them my Christmas gifts and share some Christmas dinner.

My mother singlehandedly raised all of us. She was smart and full of bright ideas – she did not even need Google (yes, there was no Google before) to think of sending my older sister to Australia to join pen pal writing and date an Australian man, which I remembered they went to an office for. I am thankful my sister followed my mother in this. It was my mother who had the idea to migrate to Australia. Maria was one of the early Filo (Filipino) migrants in the '80s in Australia, and we were all sponsored after.

I did not have a clue of how a loving husband or a loving couple was when I was a child. I met Bruce through his brother, who was in my group of friends. Bruce was very quiet and always in their house, so I was surprised that he said hi while I was walking in the neighbourhood. I said hi back.

Our next encounter was when I passed by their house on my way to the store. He asked me if I wanted to learn table tennis. I said OK. Looking back, I was so naïve when I met him; I was 14, he was 16.

As I look back, using my wisdom from all the education and life lessons I had in the 52 years of my life, my ex-husband's personality was a bit alarming when I met him. He won't talk to any of my friends or join his brother when he mingled with us. He seemed to be a loner type.

Now if I were to rewind my life, I would not even date him! Why? He is totally different from me. I do know that opposites attract, but not if they're too different. He seemed to be hiding some feelings or issues that gave me a hunch about why he was a silent type. Why? Only he would know what happened to him.

I am not after finding the reason why he abused me for so long. In the same breath, I have the answer as to why I stayed abused: I did not know I was being abused. I did not identify it as abuse. How would I know when I was a child then? I was 15. I was carrying a precious baby, and I decided to focus my attention on her instead of thinking about why and how Bruce was like that. I hid it early in the marriage.

But, so they say now, there is no excuse for abuse or bad behaviour. We should not put up with it. We are meant to have a harmonious and loving relationship.

I wish my mother had one. I wish she died having a loving relationship. I wish my mother died with someone who truly loves her. I wish a loving man loved her as much as she loved to a fault.

HAIL MY MOTHER!

These wishes of mine never came true. She died abused. On her death certificate, it says:

Cause of death: Old age, died of severe depression.

When I saw that, I asked myself how she could die of that when I knew my mother was so full of life, so happy. She would laugh at all the Filipino movies she was watching whenever she visited me in the Philippines.

Sad to say, she witnessed the abuse my ex-husband did to me.

After my flamenco dance recital, as I climbed the stairs to our fifth-floor penthouse with my mother and my children, we found out that there was no electricity. I called the house guard and asked why there was no electricity.

"Ma'am Brenda, Sir Bruce turned it off and told us not to turn it on," the guard answered, his voice trembling and posture tense as if his Sir Bruce was in front of him.

"I better go to your brother's place; it will be too hot. *Hay*, why is he like that?" my mother said, frustrated. She left to sleep at my brother's place that night.

Hail my mother! As I was looking back at this story, it was my mother who taught me to just put everything aside.

If I were my mother, and I saw my daughter being controlled like that by removing the basic need of electricity, I would have warned her of this red flag. "What do you think? Is it normal for a husband to do that?" I would ask, making my daughter think if this is abuse or not, and I would try to bring her to the reality of what a loving husband is.

Oh, hail my mother. Thank you so much. If only I could hug you today, because I am seeing the light of my story.

These are samples of intergenerational trauma unknowingly passed to each family member. My mother was abused by my father, who was an alcoholic. Maybe my mother's mother was also treated like a misnomer, disrespected by her own children at some point. Who knows? But, I promised my mother that I will cut the intergenerational trauma of being abused by a man.

I will never be abused, Mum. I am sure you are watching me and Bea in heaven. I promise that you will see me happy with a loving man who will treat me right.

Mother knows best!

My mother is simply the best in my and Arabella's eyes!

I am my mother's daughter: Breaking the intergenerational trauma

Hearing this story about me and my mother, tying up the knots to my present situation with me and my adult daughters, all these have connections. They are intertwined, woven together now in my life stories. Not one part is not connected. Although I hated the part where I stayed too long in an abusive marriage, this is the same part that made me clear the path to my freedom.

My mother may have died without someone who loved her on her side. But I think, in my heart of hearts, she died contented, as she was very religious.

I would like to share the speech

SAVING ARABELLA

In March 2022, I delivered at the International Women's Day at Wollondilly Shire Council, where I presently live, to show you that I broke the patterns of intergenerational trauma that happened to me, my mother and my daughters.

Wollondilly International Women's Day Celebration: Break the Bias

Good morning, dear Wollondilly locals and distinguished guests.

I am pleased and honoured to be here today with you in solidarity of uplifting women empowerment and gender equality in our society.

My three focal points in my speech today:

- Women forging change, walking away from domestic violence!
- Women's mental health support
- Women's marital status

I am a Wollondilly local woman who rose above from years of breaking the bias of being abused for 24 years and becoming a free, liberated and empowered woman.

I have broken the bias. I had suffered misogyny! What the heck of a word is that? It simply means woman hater!

This is my story of how I rose on my own as a woman breaking the bias to run away from an abusive, controlling, manipulative ex-husband of 24 years. It was hard, but I rescued myself and my youngest daughter from further effects of domestic violence. I rebuilt my life here in Australia.

My story is just a part of me now. Being me is my whole heart, breaking the bias of being free from men who are coercively controlling, manipulative and mentally abusive!

One, being beautiful or not is not a gauge of whether a man will marry you and love you … I am breaking the bias of what my ex-husband said to me – I am beautiful, but no one loves me. No one likes to marry me! Who cares now? I don't give a damn if someone marries me or not! I will never beg a man to marry me; I know my worth!

Anyway, going back to my story: It was a cycle of control, manipulation, verbal, physical, emotional and psychological abuse for 18 years out of 24 years! I knew deep inside my heart that I was mistreated, though I had a car, a nice house to live in with my children and my perpetrator!

At 15, I got married in church. Although my mother was adamant on the eve of my wedding, she told me, "You were supposed to be with me in Australia; you already have your permanent residence."

I just told her, "Mum, I will visit you often. I promise to finish college, and my future husband and his parents said they will look after me."

My mother's instinct was right. I **should** have gone with her.

After I graduated uni, he said, "You graduated four years, but nothing will happen to you; you don't have a job!"

I had a nice teaching career at a prestigious Catholic school.

I was in a cyclical mental dilemma in my sleep for 18 years, thinking about when this verbal and mental abuse would end.

"You are nothing without me. You will be passed from man to man and treated like a pig if you leave me." This was said constantly.

When I resigned from my 13-year teaching career, he verbally abused me and said I would be using his money and be a burden to him – this time, with all my children hearing it.

Why did I resign? It was throwing the abuse.

How did I cope with this? I compensated by learning psychology, understanding personality disorders and analysing his behavioural patterns to protect me and my children. I got attached to it! I got attached unknowingly to the day-to-day abuse of control and manipulation, and I did not even know how to escape. All I know is that I have to protect my children.

For survival, I never told anyone I was abused. In front of society, he was the Mr. Nice Guy but whispers to me, "You are nothing without me; they won't talk to you without me."

I was too scared to rock the boat. I was too scared my children would be taken away from me, as I saw some prominent actresses and rich women who walked away from their abusive husbands and ended up losing their kids. This always stuck with me that it might happen to me; if I escape, I might lose my children.

I stayed being abused rather than losing my children. I will do everything to protect them. Although for years I have been planning to leave, I didn't have courage.

Now, during multiple visits here in Australia, my mother-in-law and ex-husband continued to control my travels. I was still too scared, too attached to the abusive cycle. You never can escape being attached to your abuser for the protection of yourself and your loved ones.

I had no voice. I was kept from money, bank accounts and marital properties owned by both me and my ex-husband. The coercive control even went to basic things I loved to do and my hobbies, like dancing. When I got sick, he didn't even bother to visit me in the hospital.

Now, I know you're thinking about how I left and what I did to be free. It was when I was turning 40, and after so much psychology and learning studies, I started to have the courage and grit to be free. I felt in the fibres of my being that the shaking nerves, emotional outburst and marital distress were already in me. I planned my escape just in the nick of time, before I had a mental nervous breakdown!

He controlled the family courts. Paid all solicitors and the police. I am still legally married to him overseas. But here, as empowered as I am, I filed my divorce, and I'm so happy to say I am not legally married to him anymore here in Australia.

He removed the marital household management from me and made me a misnomer in the house. My adult kids told me they are in charge of household financial management. I was set aside.

Adding more hurt, he had kept a mistress. They had a daughter almost the same age as my youngest daughter. The mistress was seven months pregnant when I gave birth to my youngest daughter. He had to tell my big kids when the mistress was dying. The mistress died of cancer in 2015. He used sympathy to buy my kids, to accept the child in the family. Thank God we were already here.

The last abuse was my youngest daughter being taken away from me as a mother, just to take away the marital power rights from me with all the properties we have. He made me a misnomer to my big children to control the properties that are supposed to be divided equally.

"Beware, your adult children will start abusing you, will do the same control and manipulation as what your husband did to you", a psychotherapist warned me.

She was totally right.

The last abuse was my youngest daughter being taken away from me as a mother. My second eldest daughter went to me, saying she had enrolled her little sister to preschool, that she is in charge of raising her and her finances and that I shouldn't go to her school anymore.

I asked her, "Who told you that?"

I AM MY MOTHER'S DAUGHTER

"My dad told me that."

A psychiatrist warned me, after three hours of recounting my story with her, to walk away as far as I could, as he has a manipulating and controlling disorder and uses people to pry and put trouble on me. All of us – my children and I – are all victims of this gruesome, controlling, manipulating perpetrator of a husband.

My adult children told me that they would lose their inheritance if I get my share. How can a mother handle their own children being used for her abuse? It's not their fault! It's dictated by their father.

This is the cycle of domestic violence. The abuser uses the children to abuse the wife more. I am exceptional for saving myself and my youngest daughter from further mental torture and significant harm.

I will never abandon my motherhood for my youngest daughter. I take pride in having joy in raising her. I really fought to be strong for her.

Before we left, she was diagnosed by a child psychologist with separation anxiety for fear of being taken away from me. The effects of domestic violence were slowly getting into my youngest daughter, so I planned my escape.

Thinking how I escape?

Six months after my eldest daughter wanted surrogate care of my youngest daughter, I got all the courage once my one property sold. In 10 days we were here in Australia. I flew back to Australia to join my family of origin – my mother, brothers and sisters who have lived here for years.

I remember how little my youngest daughter was at 4. I carried her at the port of entry at Sydney Airport, teary-eyed, looking at her tiny eyes, "We're free now, my dear daughter."

I have reaped the effects of the residual abuse from my ex-husband. All my ex-husband's verbal abuse, I threw it here in Australia. Unknowingly. It is ingrained. I even attracted another shadow of my ex-husband. My ex-partner here abused me as well and said the same thing – that I would end up in the street when I leave him.

He is an alcoholic, which got the better of him. He told me he wanted to be single; after being sober the next day, he would want me back. He screamed and shouted at me, asking for money, and threatened to kill me. "The police won't believe you," he said. "You're not Australian."

I stopped giving my share of $200/week, as I didn't have money since my work is only Casual Relief Teaching in a local Wollondilly private school. It happened here – I walked and begged for food at Vinnies food pantries.

I attracted all shitty men who cheated on me and went to another woman right in front of me, hugging each other. Men who are noncommittal, would love-bomb and promise a marriage but would be gone after using me. I went from house to another house, not knowing that I was just projecting the mental torture that was ingrained in me by my ex-husband. Sadly, at my poor expense of persecution.

I AM MY MOTHER'S DAUGHTER

I never wanted a single thing that happened to me – being abused by men here in Australia. I was helpless … until the Victims Services of the Department of Justice helped me after I was granted as a victim of my ex-partner here who abused me. They gave me extra hours of counselling. The Department of Justice paid for my counsellor from Sydney, who is an expert in attachment and addiction. I had more than 66 hours and more than four years of counselling here to address my attachment to a toxic, abusive relationship, my mental trauma and my post-traumatic stress anxiety from domestic violence. I got better with healing the effects of intimidation by my ex-partner here.

My mother passed away in 2019. During the funeral, I still had the effects of control that the family had abused me, tried to set me aside and physically attacked me. I have been strong in having boundaries for people who try to control and manipulate me. I have developed tools to battle my anxiety. I have my self-confidence back, to listen and follow my gut feel by making sure I am safe.

I have come a long way. I was suicidal before, but not now.

I have conquered myself through a series of counselling, self-care and self-love!

My mother probably took care of me and my youngest daughter, rubbing elbows with God in heaven to make sure I have help here along the way, as I was on my own when she passed away.

I stood in dignity! Healing is taking place here.

I have been recently diagnosed as a hypervigilant by a psychologist; meaning, I am always on the lookout if someone is following me, thinking they may be paid by my ex-husband to put trouble on me. But I was taught by my counsellor that it's OK to have that. I just need to recognise and let go when it comes.

This is breaking the bias of women with mental health issues – it is alright to have mental health issues, as long as you ask for help. Don't be afraid to ask for help, and do some hard work of loving yourself.

As advised by my counsellor, I've been walking for more than two years now and finishing 10,000 steps. I noticed a great effect on my mental well-being. I get more chill and have the feel-good hormones after my walk. I joined Overcomers Outreach to help me heal my attachment to toxic, abusive relationships.

I had nothing. I didn't get my marital share except for one lone property, but I have my **self-dignity** back.

Wow, I made it! I broke the bias now. Although I have suffered mental health issues out of this shit, I came out good. My counselling and therapy taught me tools and mindfulness, self-talk, mental hygiene, and just simply being in the present and being mindful that I am safe. Yes, a lot of self-assurance is what I learned to bring back my self-worth.

Yes, I have done a lot of hard work, spending time in counselling.

So, if any one of you is suffering from mental health issues – be it anxiety or simple worry or depression or mental trauma

– please, please don't be shy to ask for help! Don't let yourself suffer too long!

Suffering is optional in life! I was so shy to get help before, but not now! Help is on the way, mateship. We are all going to make it!

I am safe here! I made a fresh start! I am free with my youngest daughter! This is enough for me till I die here in Australia.

Wondering if someone said, "You're beautiful. I love you, and I will marry you!"? No one has found me yet, but I am not worried! I believe someone is set to be my future husband. I will never beg a man to marry me; I know my worth.

I have broken the bias of all the mental and verbal abuse I suffered, and now I'm back to teaching in primary at a local school and very happy and proud about it. I am now financially independent and have broken the bias that you won't survive without a man helping you.

Now all the verbal and mental abuse of my ex-husband, I have proven here in Australia are all rubbish! The police have looked after me when I was in panic and shock in 2017 after my ex-partner abused me, proving a point that what my ex-husband and ex-partner said that the police wouldn't believe in me wasn't true at all.

Now I rise above it! I broke the bias! I am breaking the bias as a schoolteacher, teaching my students that girls can do men's jobs as well, and boys can play with dolls too.

I broke the bias by being here in front of you, rising above my story! I plant the seed with you now. Take the seed with you! Nurture it, let it grow in love, and inspire other women that they ought to be heard and shine equally as men do!

My mum is looking down in heaven now, smiling at me, "Go, Bren. I'm proud of you."

And I say, I don't give a shit about this anymore!

Wow, women power! Breaking the bias!

Thank you, everyone. I'm humbled and honoured to share my story with you.

The audience clapped when I said in my speech that I am divorced here in Australia already! How magnanimous are the lovely Australian women of Wollondilly! They felt for me as I read my speech. I was crying and my hands were shaking, but I delivered.

I was also honoured that during this day, Auntie Karen read the song of Helen Reddy, 'I Am Woman'. It was so full of meaning when it was read by Auntie Karen, who is a representative for the First Nations Australians.

I rise! I am my mother's daughter. I have come to terms with breaking the patterns of intergenerational trauma abuse in my family and my mother's story.

A poem I made for my mother.

MOTHER

I would start by saying that my mum is very spiritual and religious.

Before she goes out of the house, she would look at her 'The Eye' of Jesus photo frame and pray.

I saw her praying in her sleep, until her twilight years in the nursing home. Her eyes closed, with her hands clasped together in prayer.

I knew she was at peace, happy and contented before she left us.

As she always tells us when we are about to leave, "*Dito lang ako*!" ("I'll be here!")

She never wants to go out of the nursing home anymore, a proof that she loved her routines and was comfortable and serene.

Her way of life is her spirituality.

She walked the talk!

She was so loving of humanity that she helped a lot of people, always in service.

She received an Outstanding Volunteer Award, serving aged Australians for 20 years as a migrant volunteer and shook the hand of former Prime Minister John Howard and Former MP Parliament Pat Farmer, one of her major awards in life.

SAVING ARABELLA

I AM MY MOTHER'S DAUGHTER

My mother's Eulogy I delivered during her Funeral in January 2019

A tribute to my mother

My mother was my catalyst for change. I share with you part of my eulogy that I had read at her funeral service.

Psalm 18:32–33. "It is God who arms me with strength and keeps my way secure. He makes my feet like the feet of the deer; he causes me to stand on the heights."

We are gathered here to pay tribute to the wonderful life Corazon had on this earth. My mum, for sure, is happy seeing all of you here, showing love and respect for her as we celebrate Mum meeting our Divine Creator – God!

I am Brenda, the youngest daughter of Corazon. I share my being youngest with my twin brother – me being just five minutes older.

Mother knows best! I'm privileged to be her daughter, indeed! It's a long journey now. I am very honoured and humbled to deliver her eulogy!

I am sure she is happy that we are mostly complete with six of us of her seven children.

God must have his mysterious ways! I know my mum will go straight to heaven, for she is a firm believer of God. She was born and bred Catholic, having a Spanish parent from the Philippines.

I would like to focus on three things about my mum:

1. Her spirituality and way of life, loving Jesus
2. Her greatest values and how we all got it to succeed in life
3. Her greatest trophies and awards in life

I would start by saying that my mum is very spiritual and religious. Before leaving the house, she would look at her The Eye Jesus photo frame and pray. I saw her praying in her sleep until her twilight years in the nursing home. Her eyes closed, with her hands clasped together in prayer.

I knew she was at peace, happy and contented before she left us.

As she always tells us when we are about to leave, *"Dito lang ako!"* ("I'll be here!"). She never wanted to go out of the nursing home anymore – a proof that she loved her routines and was comfortable and serene.

Her way of life is her spirituality. She walked the talk! She was so loving of humanity, that she helped a lot of people and was always in service.

Her best friend for 50 years, Cora, who had the privilege to see my mum in her last breath, witnessed the kindness and godliness of my mum. She is here with us, and I would like to acknowledge and thank her for looking after my mum. Truly, friends are soul gifts from God!

The greatest values she had are resourcefulness, unconditional love and care, and respect for human dignity. Her stewardship was at par excellence as a single mum! She had the never-say-die-never-give-up spirit! Even in her heartbreaks, she would easily pick up herself and move on. She is a fighter!

Since Friday when she died, I slept at my eldest sister Mary's house for three nights. I listened to the stories of my mums' triumphs, struggles, joys and hardships turned into winning moments.

My mum fended for her seven children on her own as a single mum. Mum had impeccable social skills, that she would go home with money to buy food for her five children at that time.

Mary told me that Mum is resourceful in finding ways and solutions for her daily issues as a mother to her seven children. In Tagalog, *maabilidad*! Mum is full of life skills, work values and ethics. She borrowed money but never forgot to pay it and always had the dignity and integrity to manage her life well.

Her greatest trophies and awards: Her seven children. She made sure her children graduated with a bachelor's degree, as Mum was not able to finish herself but was impressively intellectual in nature.

I thank all my five older siblings for looking after Mum's needs and also all of us, taking up Mum's role to care for us – me and my twin.

The nurses in the nursing home would ask me, "Are you the daughter of Corazon? The teacher?" I would say yes. My mum was proud of me when I showed her my certification last November passing as an official NSW-accredited teacher

I think I have the facts to say my mum was the most intelligent. We use Google to check things now, but she didn't have Google in the 85 years of her life. She thinks of solutions to problems in her own logical way, backed up by her faithfulness to Christ to pray for all her intentions and goals in life and have strength to put it into action.

True to the fact, she is the brightest amongst all of us. My mum is very good in conflict resolutions. She indeed had a good track record of social, mental, emotional and physical skills.

My mother is full of vibrance, enthusiasm and positive spirit.

She did not die in vain!

My mum was a great, top-notch mum. An eloquent speaker as well as high in convincing power with great people skills. She passed all those immigration interviews on her own, without any migration agent way back in the '80s. She knew how to fill up legal migrant papers,

We are here to celebrate my mother's colourful life. Most of all, to know what kind of a mother and woman she is.

She is a strong, kind, loving, caring and resourceful mum.

My mum never played favourites, and she made sure the seven of us are loved and cared.

I know it is a bit long to mention the achievements of her children. But if my mum would be asked, she would say the same thing, mentioning the achievements of her children one by one.

I AM MY MOTHER'S DAUGHTER

Our mother gave all of us the inheritance of good values, such as perseverance, resourcefulness, kindness, hard work, love for humanity, dignity and selflessness, that we may use in the hurdles of life,

All my brothers and sisters will carry on all the values that our mother has taught us.

As we now know that Mum will celebrate her new life in Heaven!

We may all feel sad for her untimely demise. All of us siblings would like to prolong her life, feed her more so she can recover. But it is God who said, "Corazon, it is time for you to enjoy. You have done a great job on earth. Come on, lets party here now! But you made it!"

Mum is surely having a first-class business trip and destination to heaven!

After I finished my Eulogy, the audience clapped and I felt that they are actually clapping upon hearing the achievements of my mum when I shared her life through her Eulogy.

I still feel my Mum guiding me up to now. She has a big photo in my lounge where I always see and say hello to her and at times talk to her while looking at her photo in my lounge.

We got this, Mum. Thanks for always guiding and praying for me here as a single mum of Bea.

I still remember what you said to me, *"Ingatan mo si Bea. Baka kunin 'yan ng ama niya."* ("Take care of Bea. She might be taken by her father.")

I knew my mother's instinct was always right. I have protected and looked after Bea very well.

But my mother had her own fear as well, as she told me the story that when my father died, his brother came to visit us (me and my twin) as his niece and nephew.

My mother hid us on the roof where we used to rent in Makati so when my uncle came, my mother just said, they are not here at the moment.

My mother told me that she was fearful that my uncle will take us to America.

So this is the pattern of inter-generational trauma of fear that I have to cut to my family.

But I know, I am very safe here in Australia with Bea (Arabella). The Australian government have looked after us with so much human dignity and utmost care. Thanks a million, my beloved beautiful home Country, Australia.

An Empty Christmas Eve

Christmas eve of 2013. It was only me and Bea. We had dinner. Pieces of ham and rice we shared.

Empty fridge! Wow! I opened the fridge, and it was all empty except for water jugs. Not even one piece of food was there. I took a photo and sent it to my third daughter, Ann 111, then rang her.

"Why did you not go to the grocery when you knew you would be spending a week with your father, and it will just be me and Bea?"

"Oh, Mum, Dad said I can't go to the grocery yet, and the credit card is not with me." Ann 111 said.

"Wow, so you want us to go hungry for several days while you are all with your dad."

After I hung up the phone, I took a photo of the empty fridge and posted it on Facebook. This was what we have – an empty fridge with ice in the freezer and water jugs. Not even a block of butter was there! It was pure white as snow when you looked at the fridge. I rang my eldest daughter about this.

"You have to come here and go to the grocery to buy something", I told her.

"Mum, I will do something", my eldest daughter told me.

Bing! "Mum, I will meet you at the grocery tomorrow. Just drive up with Bea there", my daughter texted.

Bea and I then went upstairs to go to sleep in my room. I turned on the aircon to 18 degrees as Bea wandered around in the other room next door.

"Mum, look at the cat!" Bea called from the other room.

I ran to the room and saw that the cat had given birth in the cupboard, and she was carrying them one by one through her mouth.

"Mum, why is the cat eating her kitten?" Bea asked.

"No, Bea. She is moving them to a safer place", I answered.

"Oh!"

It was a deja vu feeling, seeing a cat protect her kittens. This is how I feel with Bea. I wanted to protect her. I had to plan my plea, my escape from this dungeon. Escape from this cell of food and petrol rations, just so my ex-husband can show he is the Bruce Almighty, powerful god! (For me, a devil Bruce Almighty act!)

As I turned the lights off, I put my palms together and prayed. "God, please take me and Bea out of here now. This is so much suffering for me and her. We are like puppets having to follow whatever her father says to my adult children. I can't take it anymore; my adult kids are telling me off and are the ones in charge of this house and not me anymore. This is breaking my heart."

I finished my prayer and smoothed Bea's hair up and down. "We'll make it, Bea," I whispered to her. "One day we'll be free from this hell."

Bea and I slept the night of Christmas Eve hugging each other.

I still remember the day that my eldest daughter laid all the money on the bed, labelled and categorised. "Here. This is for food and groceries, for petrol and the car, and for my siblings' school allowance." I passed by and happened to look. Before even asking what that was, she looked at me and said, "Mum, I got money from Dad, but you have nothing here. You have to find work and be the one to look after yourself."

I said nothing! I looked at her and went to my room, just next to where they were. I was shocked. Wait! I was a school teacher for 13 years. I took them with me and drove them to school, where I also teach. I paid for their tuition fees through my employment's educational scholarship benefits.

For the first time, I did not cry, but I said to myself that I would never forget this scene. My adult kids have been used by their father to abuse their own mother. There was not a day that I did not pray I would be saved from this day-to-day control, where it was already my adult kids who were doing the control and manipulation. I became a misnomer in the family by being stripped out of financial household management since I decided to leave Bruce. Their father used our kids to abuse and control me. It is heartbreaking.

It's Christmas day the next morning. Bea and I woke up, and I cuddled her so tight and carried her too.

"Merry Christmas, Bea. I love you." I swallowed a tiny lump in my throat as I greeted her. I could not tell her that I do not have Christmas gift for her. I did not bother to tell Bea at that time, as I saw her innocent smile and joy while the hug was tight enough for me to know she was OK without the gift.

My phone rang. "Mum, I am here in Katipunan now. I will buy you food." My eldest daughter called.

"Alright, we'll meet you there now. Thank you", I said and hung up the phone.

It was January 2014 when things started to move. It was almost my birthday, and up to now I have neither sold my one sole property nor annulled my marriage in court.

I called my ex-husband and said, "I will call the media and say that you are a tax evader."

AN EMPTY CHRISTMAS EVE

Three days later, I received a phone call from a woman who wanted to buy my property, asking if we could meet so she could have a look. It was just a flash! But it was all fabricated, planned.

"I will be taking care of the deed of sale contract. If it is alright, your ex-husband will be there in the bank when you get the payment", the buyer said. This was very strange for me, as the buy-and-sell of real estate properties in the Philippines does not normally involve the buyer preparing the deed of sale contract. It is the seller who does it. With this in mind, I knew she was a dummy buyer but never bothered with it, as I was after my freedom to plead for protection with Bea.

"He doesn't need to be there because he has power of attorney that I am allowed to sell the house", I replied.

"No, sorry. Because you are still legally married to him, he has to be there", she insisted.

I did not argue anymore. All I was thinking was how to escape this dungeon of control.

Of course, he made it hard again. He came so late to the bank. I had to go back to the property I was selling, and I started crying again on the floor for a good hour. I couldn't take that I had to see him again.

I came back to the bank as he rang that he was already there. We signed the papers. Done. I knew it was just a dummy buyer, but I said to myself, "Oh, who cares? I am free now. Bea and I can walk away now!"

Ten days later, we flew to God's country. I carried my little Bea out of Sydney Airport, teary-eyed. "We are free now, Bea!" I whispered to her. "I promise to protect you."

"Mum, *nasaan tayo*?" she asked. ("Mum, where are we?")

"We're going to your Grandma Lally, Bea. We are in Australia now." As I looked at her tiny eyes, I was teary-eyed, carrying her in my arms.

I was supposed to die when I was a baby!

"This baby girl doesn't deserve to live. I will throw her into the sea! The world is crazy, and she doesn't have a place in this crazy world!" My father angrily shouted.

My older half-brother saw my mother swimming in blood as he wrapped his 9-day-old baby sister with a blanket. "Don't you dare throw my baby sister, or I will call the townsfolk", he warned.

This cruel conversation happened when I was only 9 days old! This was only told by my older brothers when I asked them at 33 years old.

I never saw any of my baby photos nor did my mother tell any stories as to where my father was. I also did not have the courage to ask when I was a child; it was not a norm in our family to ask questions.

Now, I would like to share a connection with my faith in Jesus with this story of finding out about my dad. Jesus died at 33 – the same age I started researching about what happened to my father and my mother when I was a baby. We went to Bauan, Batangas in the Philippines to research, and it was so surprising that they still knew my father and called him by his last name, PE-tersen, in their native Batangueño accent, which sounds stronger than the Manileño accent. I remembered that vividly.

"Oh, you're the daughter of Petersen. Your father is PE-tersen! He had a motorcycle, and he was the only one with a motorcycle at that time in the '70s. *Ang puti-puti at ganda-ganda mo.*" ("You were such a beautiful white baby.")

My mother met my American father in 1970 when he was taking a vacation after being conscripted to Vietnam. After his work in Vietnam, he travelled to the Philippines to relax. He stayed in the southern part of Luzon, where he loved living, as it was near the sea.

My mother was separated from her first partner, whom she had five kids with. She was single when she met my father. Much as I like to tell stories about my childhood or me being a baby, my mother never told me any story about me as a baby and my father.

As I was growing up, as young as 7 or 8 years old, I heard the neighbours whispering, "How come she has a different last name from her brothers and sisters?"

I WAS SUPPOSED TO DIE WHEN I WAS A BABY!

"Anak sa labas 'yan!" ("She's an illegitimate child!")

This is how Filipinos treat children with different family names. The Philippines has a stigma if your family name is different from your other siblings. I kept this story from my mother and my older siblings up to now. I never knew how to express my feelings before. I just always tucked myself in bed, in tears, thinking, *Why are they saying that about me? Why do I have a different last name from my other siblings? Can my mother just change it? Where is my dad?*

These were all the questions I had growing up with a social stigma of being immoral for having a different last name. Don't blame me for thinking that. The Philippines is a patriarchal society with no divorce law aside from a non-prejudicial annulment, which means spouses have to prove to court that they can no longer live together.

Growing up with this stigma gave me a hard time to always assert myself in the early years of marriage, as I did not want to have a broken marriage. The inner child in me would say, "But you had that, and you hated it when you were younger. Please don't let your kids experience what you hated when you were a child."

All I wished for when I was a child was to have a happy family. What does that honestly mean? Now, thinking as an adult, how in the world would I know the concept of a happy family when I never experienced one? Maybe I just imagined it and pictured it out in my brain at that time.

As a child I was always active, playing with my best childhood friend, Leila. She is the only fond memory I have of my childhood. I remember playing more with her than with my twin brother. We always fought as siblings, and he loved to help my older siblings fold clothes and clean the house, anyway.

They told me I was tomboyish, always climbing the street's *kamias* tree with Leila. She had a *palayok lutu-lutuan*, a toy crock pot easily found in any market in the Philippines. We would pound leaves, pour water on them, and pretend we were cooking. Oh, there was a time we did cook natural food in that pot! We had charcoal underneath, and we cooked soup. We never had any technology; instead, we ran around and played all day.

I was always at Leila's house, from the time I woke up until dinner time. If I was lucky, which was always, her mother would make me stay for dinner – and I loved the cooking of her mother.

Leila and I were neighbours in a three-door apartment with cars parked just beside. As soon as the cars were out, we would be happy to run around and play *patintero* (or block the runner), cops and robbers or hide and seek all day. We also played all the girlie stuff such as Chinese garter, jackstone, paper dolls and tea set cooking stuff.

Leila and I were like sisters. I remember wearing her Scholastican uniform once, wishing that I had studied in the same Catholic school as her. I did study in a Catholic school, but it's not an exclusive school for girls. The tuition fee was a lot cheaper, and my mom couldn't afford to pay for the exclusive school where Leila was.

The saddest day of my life came when Leila had to move to a suburb in another city. Naturally, I lost contact with her. Years later, in 1996, I ended up applying as a school teacher at St. Scholastica's

I WAS SUPPOSED TO DIE WHEN I WAS A BABY!

College, Leila's old school, and enrolled my eldest daughter in kindergarten. I volunteered every dismissal and wore the parent volunteer uniform, which was a denim vest with *Bantay Bata* (Child Watch) written on the back.

I was vacationing in Australia in 1996 and attended the wedding of my sister when the school rang me for a substitute teaching job interview. I rang the school straight in the morning after I returned home. "Hi, this is Ms Petersen. I'm interested to be a substitute teacher, but I was overseas when you rang."

I came for the interview. I was just 25 then. I vividly remember the principal who welcomed me with so much warmth and hospitality. "Hi, Brenda. I heard that you like to be a teacher. You know, I like teachers who chose to be teachers, like you. You are a teacher by choice, as you are one of the parents who decided to be a teacher here. I like that."

"I may not be the best teacher, but I will do my best. I have the passion to teach, and I want to grow and learn more here." I replied.

Voila, I got the job!

I came home happy that day. Remembering that my husband told me I wouldn't find a job and that I was a bum, I said to him in jest that I got the teaching job. Yet, he did not even congratulate me or even give me a gift. I heard nothing from him.

Going back to that story now as an adult with my wisdom, I would definitely assert to him and say, "I got the job. You told me I just graduated and would end up a bum!"

Who cares now? I am free, and I know the difference. Now, you will see all my sufferings are always hidden from the start.

I wonder why I didn't assert how I felt. Why did I allow things to happen to me, like being treated like a second-class woman in the house? It only became worse, and in the end I felt treated like a rug!

Serendipity! Divine providence!

I believe in divine intervention. One day, my Grade 7 student asked me, "Miss, do you know Leila Santiago?"

"Yes, of course," I replied. "She is my childhood best friend, and I have been searching for her, as I lost contact with her."

"She is my auntie, Miss", my student shared.

"Wow! Really? Can you please give my phone number?" I requested, hopeful.

Leila rang me one day, and we caught up with each other. We had a long day and night of catching up; she even went to my place to chat more.

See, all my childhood frustrations of not being able to study at St. Scholastica's College with Leila resulted in me being a teacher there and finding Leila again through one of my students. How beautiful is this story I cherished!

I WAS SUPPOSED TO DIE WHEN I WAS A BABY!

Leila always reminds me now about the last day we were together. "Remember, Bren? We were like in a movie scene; we were just hugging each other so tight and crying only because I was moving house!" Up to now, she and I are still in contact even though she is overseas. We would message and check up on each other.

Leila and I both share the same sentiments in life. She would say, "*Haaayyy*, Bren. We have the same destiny in marriage!" and we would laugh on the phone.

I would tell her, "I love you, Lei. We are both strong women and the best mums to our kids."

She would reply, "Love you too, Bren!"

Thank God for my eldest brother who saved me when I was a baby! I thank my eldest brother that at 14 years old, he had presence of mind to wrap me in a blanket and bring me to the neighbour for safety as my father wanted me to be thrown into the sea. I would not be able to tell you these beautiful stories if not for him.

The best part of my life is knowing and tying up all these loose ends. It may be a sad, traumatic event for my mother, which was why she cannot even tell me that story. So, I am thankful to the Australian government that I was able to share precious years with her and visit her at her nursing home and ask for stories about her and my dad.

See what Australia brought to our family? Healing took place to my mother as I asked her, "Mum, tell me some stories about my dad, please."

"'Yung daddy mo may motorsiklo. Diyos ko, ang bilis magpatakbo!" she shared in our native language. ("Oh, your father had a motorcycle and, God forbid, he rides it so fast!")

"There was a time I was riding with him, and then we went to this top of the mountain. The view was so beautiful! I saw so many green trees. The province was so breathtaking. The air was fresh, soothing me as I rode in your dad's bike."

I was smiling and teary-eyed as I listened to her. Had I known that story as a child, I could have known what a loving couple was. I had the grace to have that photo with her and my dad on the motorcycle. This was my putting the puzzle pieces together.

My childhood may have been full of sorrow except for my days with Leila. I still remember that I was compared to my twin. I was so bad at maths, and my brother-in-law would teach me

I WAS SUPPOSED TO DIE WHEN I WAS A BABY!

until the wee hours just so I could learn. It stuck in my brain that I was dumb and my twin was brighter than I was until I grew up. It is true – he was a lot brighter than me when we were both in school. Honestly, I did not mind but, unknowingly, I developed a hatred for maths and had so much maths anxiety growing up.

When I took the Teacher Licensure Examination in the Philippines, I made sure I answered all the science, English, history and current events, geography and professional occupation tests. But during the maths questions, I was not too confident. The mental trauma I suffered was too deep, that my then husband told me, "You're a teacher, but you don't know how many zeros there are in millions? Oh, *sige nga. Ilang* zeros *meron sa isang milyon*?" ("You're a teacher, but you don't know how many zeros there are in millions? Go ahead. How many zeros does a million have?")

When he asked me that, I just looked at him and did not even answer. All his verbal abuse was slowly creeping into my veins, my brain cells, my nerves and my whole body that I was always mentally blocked every time he would mentally and verbally abuse me. As I grappled to walk away, my nerves were shaking. This also made me plan my escape, as my mental health was already giving up. I was just crying and crying.

Indeed, Australia is God's country, as I even became a maths teacher here and fell in love with maths. Now I can say that I can teach it and not hate it anymore. Maths is life, and life is maths. We see maths everywhere – as soon as we wake up, we check the time, we make sure to measure the scoop of coffee and the directions to go to work. I share this with my students every time I hear them say, "Miss, I am not good at maths."

Thank you from the bottom of my heart, Australia, for the love, for the mateship, for the utmost care and for all the counselling and therapy you gave me.

"Listen to me, and after we finish our work, we will have a brain break music. I will sing and dance for you." I make sure my maths lessons are fun and engaging.

These stories are just testimony that I was able to rise above all the struggles, hardships of the trauma I had in my abusive marriage.

I wish my dad and mum had marriage counselling before, but alcoholism got the better of my dad instead. He pushed my mother from the second floor after she gave birth to me. I was just 9 days old. My mother ended up staying in the hospital for nine months, and my twin and I had to stay in the nursery room, as no one will look after us.

In 2004, when I was 33 years old, I walked into a small, old birthing centre. "Hello, I am Brenda. I am looking for a document about my birth here." I asked in my native language.

"Here, I will show you the registration book." As the attendant flipped the big, old, yellowish book, my eyes widened, and I got goosebumps from head to foot, surprised by the deja vu feeling to see the signature of my father that he was checking in my mother to give birth there. This disproved what my ex-husband has been saying all along, that I was born popped out from a bubble, that I don't have a father and that my mother was a slut.

I was there as a baby. I was so happy, and I didn't even cry but just made sense of my childhood stories. It's a big deal when I say

I WAS SUPPOSED TO DIE WHEN I WAS A BABY!

I didn't cry, as I easily cry and am very emotional.

To my dad, I forgive you for trying to throw me into the sea to kill me. If you had psychological help, you would have been a great dad and a loving partner to my mother.

Sadly, at 33 years old, my father passed away in 1971 on his way to Manila to visit my mother in the Philippine Orthopedic Hospital and say sorry for what he had done and to bring us all to America, including my elder siblings.

He was drunk while riding his motorcycle and crashed into a truck that was parked.

I am sad about this story. I wish I had met my dad. In the same breath, I am happy to know his story to tie this up with my goal to break the pattern of intergenerational trauma that happened in my family.

No to an alcoholic partner for me – I should say that now as I see this story unfolding.

See if this intergenerational trauma pattern stopped in the next coming chapters.

I will leave you here to guess whether I really did get that lesson to not attract an alcoholic man.

The world is not crazy after all!

My dad, I wish to tell you that the world is beautiful!

Dad, I tell my students that we ought to make this place a better world to live in. And they loved it. I introduce myself as Ms Petersen, with a heart in the end, and I can't change it; it's there. We are all interconnected no matter where we come from. No matter what colour, size or shape we have. My students agree and nod with a smile every time they hear this. "That's nice, Miss," they would say.

Thanks, Dad, for all the lessons you gave me. I want you to know that I feel you are always watching me from heaven with my grandma, your mother, from heaven. I actually look like my grandma, judging from the photos my cousin Bridgit gave me.

I wish to tell you that my Father God had always kept me company, that I never longed for a father image while I was growing up. I guess you rubbed elbows with God to make sure I was alright with all this crazy world that you were talking about.

By the way, Dad, you were kind of right – I experienced some craziness in this world, but don't worry. I got this!

Love you, Dad. I wish one day you can visit me in my dream.

Oh, one last hug and love to my mum there. Please rub elbows with God again, with my mum, to give me a kind, respectable, honourable Australian man. Might be too much to ask, but Australia taught me the right standards for a loving man.

Thank you for meeting up with my mum, and I am pretty sure you did love me as your beautiful daughter.

Love your beautiful daughter,
Bren

Bruce Almighty vs. the Dancing Queen

There was a movie about a man who complained that God was not doing his job properly. He asked God if he could have powers, so God granted it. But he abused and used it once for revenge.

I mentioned this movie, as there was one incident that had the same scene where the man used all his powers in bad ways. This was around 2006. My husband called me into the bedroom and said, "Sit down there at the foot of the bed." As I obliged, he continued, "*Tama na 'yang* flamenco-flamenco *na 'yan. Ibalik mo 'yung mga* tickets *na binili mo!*" ("Enough of that flamenco dancing. You are going to return all the tickets you bought!")

"Why?" I asked. "I paid for it with my own teaching salary, anyway, and it is my enjoyment. I love dancing."

"If you dance and go there, I will go to Centro Flamenco and get all the tickets you bought so no one can watch you", he threatened.

"No," I said, standing my ground. "I paid for those tickets so that my children can watch me." Not caring for his reaction, I left the room.

As I went on with my day, my phone rang, "Hi, Brenda. This is Kay, the secretary at Centro Flamenco. I am ringing because your husband is here, and he wants to get the tickets that you bought."

"Don't give it, please." I urgently warned. "I will be the one to get that from you. Thanks so much." I hung up the phone, feeling devastated. How in the world does Bruce have the time to even go to my dance school and get the tickets so no one can watch me? Yet, I stood firm in going to my flamenco dance recital no matter what happened.

The day of my recital came. I wanted to prepare early and go to my recital, so I asked our driver for my car keys. "Red, *pakiabot ng susi ng kotse*." ("Red, may I have my car key, please?")

"Ma'am, *na kay* Sir *lahat ng susi*", Red answered. ("Ma'am, Sir Bruce has all the car keys.")

Taken aback, I could only ask, "*Ha?*"

"*Wala po samin yung susi. Na kay* Sir *po lahat*", he repeated. ("We don't have the keys with us. They're all with Sir Bruce.")

BRUCE ALMIGHTY VS. THE DANCING QUEEN

I went back up the long stairs and into the fifth floor, where we live. I told my adult daughters that we couldn't go because I didn't have the car keys.

"It's OK, Mum. I will ask for my boyfriend's car to take us", my eldest daughter told me.

I said OK, I would just tell Tita (Aunty) Jenny to bring me to my recital now as I needed to go with Gilee, who was also excited in her purple Flamenco costume. Gilee was dancing Flamenco with me and the other girls who enrolled, too.

"I'll see you later at RCBC Auditorium. Make sure you bring your Lally", I told my eldest daughter, referring to her grandma, my mother who was visiting from Australia at that time.

I had all my make-up done – complete with a red lippy and fake eyelashes – and had donned my costume – red skirt with a red rose on the left side, floral, red flamenco shawl and a big red fan. I had forgotten whether my husband was coming or not. All I knew was that I was so excited to dance.

I performed two dances – belly dancing with my teacher Clara and my classmates, and flamenco fan dance, which was so regal in red! I looked liked an authentic Spanish Flamenco dancer because of my mixed race.

I danced pretty well; I am a very passionate dancer, after all! I loved dancing since I was a young girl. From 7 to 12 years old, Leila and I, and her brothers plus my twin, would practice dancing in the garage for our yearly Christmas dance performance in the garage. This was always a big event in school every Christmastime.

Leila's eldest sister would choreograph our dance, and we'd wear matching costumes – denim pants and white shirts paired with white and red striped knee-high socks for girls, and white and blue knee-high socks for boys. Sometimes we wear polka dot dresses for good luck to welcome the new year.

When I became a teacher, I was a dancer teacher too. I had always joined cheer dancing at my school, and I was also one of the best dance teachers. When I resigned after 13 years of service at St. Scholastica's College, the school president, Mother Angelica Leviste, OSB, told me as I said goodbye in her office, "Oh, Brenda. I am going to miss your dancing. You were really good in cheer dancing."

BRUCE ALMIGHTY VS. THE DANCING QUEEN

Up to now my passion for dance never left me. Dance was my therapy when I hid my abuse in marriage. No wonder I was so strong in not following the manipulation and control of my husband to stop me from dancing. This was my only way to express myself and say, "I am so beautiful, and I just love every minute of it."

He never came to the recital. Worse, he never came home. One week, two weeks, three weeks, four weeks. No shadow of him! I started getting worried, as I would not survive feeding my children plus paying for all the bills and the salaries of our household maids and guards. I would not be able to afford it with my teaching salary.

I spoke to my eldest daughter. "I think we have to find your dad, and maybe I should talk to him to come home."

My eldest would always say, "Mum, you always take Dad back. He left. Let him come home on his own."

At this time, my eldest daughter was sensing something was going on, but I never said it. She can see it, especially when we came home from the flamenco recital.

"Red," I called out upon coming home. *"Bakit ang dilim?"* ("Why is it so dark?")

"Ma'am, *sinara po ni* Sir *'yung kuryente"*, Red told me. ("Ma'am, Sir Bruce turned off the electricity.")

I just looked at him and went upstairs with my kids. My mother was there, as I said previously.

"Mum, there is no aircon; it's too hot!" All my kids kept telling me as I was fanning them with my flamenco fan from the recital. Even when I was half asleep all night, I was still fanning them. Heat was imminent, and my kids were complaining they could not sleep at night, as it was too hot.

Then, we received a message from the house guard that their sir was coming home. My kids – Ann 1, Ann 11 Ann 111, Gilee and Benedict – and I were waiting quietly upstairs. We still did not have electricity, not because we did not pay but because the Bruce Almighty turned it off.

Our door was open, and we could see that there was no light in the staircase, from the first floor to the fifth floor.

Upon his arrival, the lights on every floor Bruce passed slowly turned on, same as the movie scene in Bruce Almighty. When he reached our floor, the house guard opened the door, carrying Toy Kingdom-wrapped gifts as my ex-husband entered!

I counted the gifts; there were only three! He gave one gift to Benedict, to Gilee and to Ann 111. Surprisingly, nothing for Ann 1 and Ann 11, who watched my recital and made sure that we had a ride through their boyfriends, thwarting his plans to control and manipulate me from enjoying my dancing!

What a cruel, manipulative and controlling husband and father he is! All this, I had to suffer. I had to swallow my hurt and pain because the little girl inside me was screaming, "No, Brenda! Don't let them experience the broken family you had! Just sacrifice." I still took him back, but the same cycle of domestic violence continued.

Well, that was my old self! Now I realise that any little control to stop me from doing things or even restricting the basic needs of children and hindering them from an easier and safer life is a sure sign of a red flag. I thank my God and Saviour for saving me, for giving me the courage to walk away.

Now, his godlike complex never stopped! In 2009, I fell pregnant again; eight years after I gave birth to my *unico hijo* (only son). I was really shocked that I got pregnant. It was just a one-off. Remember, he never asked for sex since 1993, but we would have one off when he sees me getting slimmer and busy with my dancing.

I have to share a very sensitive part of our married life that was strange and very weird. After I left him, Bruce still controlled the maintenance of all our eight cars, mine included. So, my half-brother, Gino, went in my stead to get the money for the service maintenance. This is when Bruce said to him, "I don't love Brenda anymore since the last three kids!"

Yes, we had eight cars – Ford E-150, Toyota Innova, Lancer sedan, Toyota Avanza, Vios, two Nissan Sentras and my Fortuner – before I left. He sold the Nissan Sentra when I left my marriage, as it was on the settlement. But karma bit him. The buyer was a scammer. He did not pay Bruce, according to my kids. I don't really know if it is true or not. I was able to settle a Toyota Fortuner during the negotiations. Later on, I left it there, but in 2017, after my car accident here in Australia, I had to tell my daughter Ann 111 to sell it for me so I could buy another car. She gladly sent me the money to buy a new car here.

When Gino told me this in 2011, I cried, thinking why he kept me anyway. He could have told me, and I could have gone back to my mum in 1993, after my third daughter was born.

In 1993, Bruce's mother brought me to America to give birth to my third daughter Ann 111. They were scared that my Rh-negative blood type might produce complications if I gave birth in the Philippines, where less than 1% had that blood type.

Bruce came after I gave birth, in December 1993. His Aunty Joy said, "Oh, you should go out and have overnight somewhere."

He was quiet, but he still followed his aunty. I brought my 3-month-old baby in the carrier, as she was breastfed. While we were in the hotel, he would not touch me or even talk to me!

"How come you don't miss me?" I asked. When I tried to hug and caress him, he pinched me and kicked me out of bed.

I was so embarrassed of myself that day. I was only 21 at that time. So naïve, so innocent. I didn't even know how to react.

I cried myself in bed and hugged my baby to feed her. This incident that happened in America has been happening until I left him in 2011.

I hid this sexual abuse, which is under the stages of narcissistic sexual abuse. I researched, and I quote:

> "**Sexual Withdraw.** Some narcissists completely withdraw all sex from the relationship. Any requests you make sexual abuse for sex are met with ridicule, rants about

your performance, and excessive excuses for abstinence. You are to blame for their lack of desire, it is never their fault. They will also oscillate between excessive sex and complete withdraw to maintain control and manipulate you into doing whatever they ask.

"For the narcissist, your body is theirs and their body is theirs. Therefore they feel entitled to give ultimatums about your body. You have to lose weight or exercise more or groom yourself in a certain way to keep them satisfied."*

I suffered all of this. This was totally my ex-husband.

In my case, he used sex against me, telling me "You are a prostitute. You will be a pig passed from man to man if you leave me!" He would say this every single day, sometimes in text messages too.

Every time I go near him, he would say, "Get away from me. Go to the kids and look after them."

There was no affection.

Once, he brought me to his Rotary meeting. His friends said, "Oh, your wife is so beautiful. Why are you not bringing her often? It's the first time we've seen her."

"She is my hidden treasure!" he'd say.

---

* C Hammond, The Stages of Narcissistic Sexual Abuse, Psych Central, 2015, https://psychcentral.com/pro/exhausted-woman/2015/06/the-stages-of-narcissistic-sexual-abuse.

I know that was not a compliment, because that day, and every time we were on our way to any event, he would whisper to me, "You are nothing. Your kids won't respect you. Friends only talk to you because of me, and your kids only respect you now because they are young. But when they become adults, they will only respect me. I am the one who has the money; teacher *ka lang*!" ("I am the one who has the money; you're just a teacher!")

This went on from 1988 until I left him in 2011.

The pinching and kicking out of the bed were constant every time I tried to hug him. There would be a time when he sees I am getting preoccupied with myself, like I was back with my old size 8 figure. I didn't need to take pills, as we didn't have an active sex life anyway, and he really never asked for it. We normally did withdrawal as a form of birth control.

I really feel small talking about this now. I know this story is not only about this, but I believe in the divinity of sex, which means it is the gift of God for two people who are in love and their consummation of marriage. I felt so weird about telling this before, that I never told anyone, even my friends, about it.

Many times, during our wedding anniversary, Valentine's day, or my birthday – if I was lucky – or his birthday, we would check in a five-star hotel. Guess what would happen. We would check in at around 12 pm and then he would go and say, "I have to work. I will come back at 11 pm."

I would only respond with an OK, then enjoy being alone. This went on every time we checked in a hotel, So it was just for show, to be seen as a loving husband in society. I ended up not asking to go to the hotel anymore. This is very painful to share; I felt so dehumanised and belittled as a woman – left alone, kicked and punched, receiving no affection at all.

I stayed in this kind of relationship and kept this secret for years while my children were growing up. When they were growing up, I started to learn how to divert myself into dancing. Going to the spa on weekends, just on my own was a treat for me.

For 18 years out of 24 years of marriage, he went home at 2 am – sometimes even 4 am! I would call him, and he would answer in a grumpy voice, "Don't disturb me; I am working."

Yep, 1 am or 2 am and still working.

My friends from work would go to my place, as my house was a stone's throw away from the school where I teach, and stay up to 10 pm. They would ask me, "Where is your husband?"

"Working", I would answer.

"Working? What work goes on until dinner time or this late at night? This has been happening for so long, Brenda. Why don't you have him followed? *Baka may babae 'yan!*" ("Maybe he has a mistress!")

"No way! I won't waste my money to have him followed. I am too beautiful for that", I would joke.

I focused, instead, on learning family psychology and family counselling and taking my master's degrees in teaching and women studies. I studied to compensate for hiding my abuse and to learn his personality quirks – I did not yet consider his actions as abuse, as I did not know that before. I only found out that it was abuse upon my years of education and observing other normal loving relationships.

From 1986 to 2011, no one knew of all the abuse my husband has been doing to me. But my best friend, Jenny, and her sister-in-law Didi, who happens to be the school principal, knew about that abuse, as we were neighbours. They knew about my ex-husband turning off the electricity and hiding the car keys, as I went to ask their help. But that was the only extent of abuse they knew.

They never knew the trail of abuse inside the bedroom or the abuse that has been happening since 1988.

Even so, they did not like the idea that he could make me and my kids suffer by taking away my car keys and turning off the electricity.

In 2005, the fourth-grade head teacher also found out my phone was confiscated by my ex-husband when we went on a field trip. When we arrived at our destination, Ms Lazaro, the head teacher, came up to me and asked, "Bren, did you receive my announcement through text?"

I told her I did not because my husband had my cell phone. "*Kanya daw 'yun. Siya daw nagbabayad*", I reasoned. ("He says the phone is his because he's the one who pays for it.")

He would confiscate the phone, even though he's mad for nothing. He would confiscate it if I don't follow the littlest mundane thing. Once, I woke him up for a pictorial and taste testing at The

BRUCE ALMIGHTY VS. THE DANCING QUEEN

Peninsula Hotel for my second daughter's 18th birthday party. He cancelled that! My children were so sad; they were all dressed up for it.

My last straw was after our Boracay trip in April 2011. I got confined because of sunburn that became a first-degree burn; my leg muscles relaxed, and I could not walk. I needed to be confined in the hospital to replenish the potassium that was depleted from the sunburn in my leg.

Well, I did not put sunblock, but I put a suntanning lotion. (My abuse was throwing out this time and I thought of sunbathing but ended up hurting myself)

When my children rang their dad that they were bringing me to the hospital, he said, *"Perwisyo na 'yang nanay niyo. Gumastos na, nagkasakit pa!"* ("Your mother is such a burden. She already spent so much money, then even got sick!")

Hearing this, I took the phone and asked, "What did you say to the kids?"

He repeated the same thing, so I handed the phone back to my kids and told myself, "That's it. I will leave him, and I will never take him back. My kids hear all the verbal abuse, and they will not respect me anymore."

I realised that my ex-husband never loved me before. Now I realise he could not give me love, as he never knew how to love. He loved me the way he knew from his own upbringing. Now, it is not only 18 years, but I knew it started ever since we got married that I was abused.

In my wisdom now, I knew I was abused at 15. Having no power to decide as a minor and and letting the adults decide for me was wrong.

I was abused as a child.

I was neglected. I was isolated. I was curtailed with my child's human rights!

I wish Australia can hear me!

I wish God of Australia to be my refuge for the rest of my life.

I can rant about so many abuses that I suffered from my ex-husband. I passed a raw 20-page timeline of violence in the Family Court and the police in the Philippines and the Australian Immigration when I arrived in Australia in 2014.

In my wisdom now while reading the raw timeline of violence in 2011, it looked like I was so needy, although I verbalised all the abuse, but the repeating words prove that I was in marital distress.

These are the important dates and years of my domestic abuse. The dates and years will give you an idea how long I have kept the abuse.

- 1985 – My family's petition for Australian family migration was approved.
- 1986 – I got married at 15.
- 1990 – I came late from school function. I was punched in the lip for it.

BRUCE ALMIGHTY VS. THE DANCING QUEEN

1992 – I graduated but Bruce physically abused me and said that I did not have a job and that I would be a bum.

1993 – I gave birth to my third daughter in America while living at Bruce's Aunty's house.

1996–2009 – I became a teacher for 13 years at St. Scholastica's College, Manila

1998 – the fourth daughter arrived, five years after the third girl in 1993.

1999 – Verbal abuse: "You're are nothing, useless. Your bosses at St. Scholastica's College Manila don't want to make friends with you; it's only because of me and my money. Without me, they won't." In my mind, "How can it be? I am the employee there, not you."

2001 – Our fifth child came; a boy. I thought Bruce would now be a changed man by not verbally abusing me. But he was still the same: belittling acts, demeaning words. The control, verbal abuse and intimidation still continued. He said I was a slut, born out of a bubble from my mum, and that I was like my mum – a prostitute. Lawyers and the police won't believe me. He never stopped physically hurting me ever since I told his mother about it. When I ring him, he would say, *"Leche ka! Ang dami kong ginagawa."* ("Damn you! I'm doing so many things."). He kept driving me away when I try to make a conversation that we should try to bond as husband and wife.

2003–2004 – My issues regarding my failure due to absence when my professor asked me to attend a 7 Stages to Life Healing Retreat on a weekend in the Master in Family Psychology.

2006 – Major fight.

2009 – I got pregnant with Arabella. This time, I let him sign my ligation three months before I gave birth.

10 July 2009 – I drove myself to the hospital to give birth to Arabella as he was not home for three months. I rang the driver to get my car in the hospital parking lot.

11 July 2009 – I gave birth to Arabella. Bruce was there because my eldest daughter called him.

2009 – He controlled all the household employees, and it was only him allowed to have a say. He scolded me and swore at me in front of the cashier at a pharmacy store for getting some toiletries and cleaning materials.

October 2009 – 3 January 2010 – He did not come home for three months.

24 December 2009 – My children and I tried to get him to go home. He said his life is better without us.

27 December 2011 – He asked all the six kids to come. He verbally abused all my kids that day. He told Benedict that "even if he is saving money, that is nothing" in our native language. Ann 11 said it's good that they barely understand the verbal abuse they suffered.

June 2010 – March 2011 – I taught at Miriam College, 10 minutes away from where we lived.

22 January 2011 – My "Fab@40" birthday celebration at Sofitel Hotel Philippines.

February 2011 – Bruce verbally abused me that I was fat, ugly and that no man will like me. They will just weigh me and pay me to have them, like a prostitute.

March 2011 – I resigned from Miriam College (I was throwing the abuse now)

3 April 2011 – Bruce verbally abused me in front of the kids, saying that I resigned from teaching and would use my petrol money and that I was a pest, disturbance and parasite relying on him.

5–7 April 2011 – Boracay trip to chaperone my second daughter

7 April 2011 – I had a fever. I was shivering, cannot walk and crying in pain. My legs were too burnt from the beach at Boracay.

8 April 2011 – My last straw when I got sick after a sunburn that turned into a first-degree burn. He never visited me in the hospital and verbally abused me that I was a disturbance and spent his money for hospitalisation.

17 April 2011 – Economic abuse that I could not even buy ice cream for my son and daughter when they asked me.

18 April 2011 – Bruce did not come home.

18 April 2011 – Bea has no food allowance at almost 2 years old, except for milk.

21 April 2011 – The Mother Prioress of the Benedictine Sisters prayed for me and referred me to Women's Crisis Centre.

22 April 2011 – Psychotherapist counselling session. She warned me that my adult kids would control me the same way their dad did, as I stayed too long.

24 April 2011 – My adult children laid all the money on the bed and told me that I had nothing given to me and that her dad said to tell me to work (even under severe marital distress).

25 April 2011 – Bing and I went to Atty Ana Luz Cristal. Told her everything above.

25 April 25, 2011 – I photocopied all our properties' titles

29 April 2011 – My second daughter took the car keys and told me to use a manual car. I said no.

1 May 2011 – My second daughter gaslit and tried to control me to forgive her dad. She said her dad is kind and I was the abusive one.

3 May 2011 – Bruce controlled all of us not to join a family outing for Ateneo basketball friends of my son.

13 May 2011 – Economic abuse from basic food and petrol allowance to bring my kids to their drama activities. I

was warned to not go anywhere but just to bring Gilee to Rockwell for her activity; otherwise, petrol will run out and he won't give money for it.

September 2011 – Dismissed violence against women case, with three agreements, annulment and go to Australia with Bea.

November 2011 – Gave one property for the violence against women to be dismissed.

January to August 2013 – I saved money to go to Australia.

August 2013 – I visited in Sydney and informed my mother and siblings about my plan to relocate in Australia. My second daughter told me she enrolled Arabella to preschool and not to go to her school, as she was in charge of Arabella's financial management for food and ballet fees. I asked her, "Who told you that?" to which she replied, "My dad told me to tell you."

26 August 2013 – Bruce told me let Ann 1 and Ann 11 raise Bea and go to Australia alone.

December 2013 – Facebook scam; threatened to kill me.

14 February 2014 – My lone property in Makati was sold.

26 February 2014 – Arabella and I flew to Australia.

Why do you think I lasted this long? Twenty-four long years I have stayed abused. You might think I am Bruce Almighty, too – not feeling the pain for staying that long in and out of the abusive cycle, chewing the abusive words day in and day out and spitting it out the next day, as I need to drive my kids to school where I work and teach.

I was lucky enough to have free tuition fees for my daughters, as it was one of the employee benefits in an exclusive school for girls in Manila.

BRUCE ALMIGHTY VS. THE DANCING QUEEN

He would only pay the miscellaneous fees, which was not a lot.

I am saying this now, as he was such a liar in court when I was having a settlement and filed for a Violence Against Women and Children (VAWC) case in the Philippine court. I fell off the floor when the court lawyer showed me his affidavit that says, "Brenda never contributed to the marital household finances; she was just dancing."

I bursted into tears and said, "That is not fair! I was a school teacher, and yes, I was a cheer dancer in school for the 13 years I was there."

I devoted myself with my kids, while he goes home at 2 or 3 am!

There was once a burglar who broke into our house while he was not home. I was heavily pregnant with Arabella, and I had to gather all my kids to go down, as the house guard advised. We had to sleep in our other condo to be safe. All throughout, he was nowhere to be found. Thinking back, he was probably with his mistress.

In 2007, my colleague once told me, "Brenda, I saw your husband holding hands with a girl at Bon Appetit in Edsa Shangri-La mall."

"That might be his client", I defended.

When I went home, I told him in jest. "Oh, Ms Callus saw you."

"Oh, that is just the client", he answered, avoidant.

I was still naïve at that time, so I did not have a clue whether he was telling the truth or not. I had always been a secure wife – never jealous, even up to now. What I cannot take is how frigid, how controlling, how mentally and sexually abusive, and how manipulative he is.

When our computer school business grew, he started buying real estate properties. He would wake me up at 2 am, shaking me, "Sign this, Brenda", he would say as he hands me the pen.

I would be half asleep and couldn't even read what I would be signing. I would say, "I am sleepy, I have work tomorrow."

"Just sign it. I just bought some properties." He would dangle the pen on my face and would push me to sign even if I was half asleep.

That happened every time he bought properties. At times, he would go to my school at lunch break and would make me sign. Of course, I couldn't stay long, reading and signing a long contract for properties he bought.

He would simply point at the space that said "With marital consent" and my printed name, and say, "Sign here."

His coming to my workplace to make me sign is not to see me with any affection.

Some of you might like that, and say, "Oh, wow, you have a lot of properties!" But I hated those days that I had to sign; that and when he wants to bring me to the bank to roll over our loan were the only times he would be nice to me.

He would pick me up on my lunch break and bring me back to work. I honestly didn't mind those properties. I was just focused on my teaching career and my kids.

BRUCE ALMIGHTY VS. THE DANCING QUEEN

He would always want me to go with his mother for travel overseas. They made sure my first overseas travel was not to Australia; it was to America, when I was pregnant with my third child.

I was too excited when we arrived at the airport in Los Angeles.

"This is the country of my father. So exciting!" I told my mother-in-law.

"Oh, you won't be able to come here had it not been for me", she said condescendingly with a cranky voice and a frown.

I just said nothing and became quiet for a while. I only said something about my dad. What was wrong with it that she became angry?

Going back to that story now, I think she didn't want for me to connect with any of my blood relatives; she wanted me isolated. Call a spade a spade – I was locked in a dungeon, which I only knew after I left the abusive marriage.

I cannot believe that I am writing all this now. This is so surreal for me. I was just struggling to go here in Australia in 2011. I was so weak to work. I was in marital distress. I resigned from my high school teaching job when I thought I just wanted a change. It was the hidden abuse throwing out.

In 2011 I celebrated my 40th birthday. I told my husband I wanted to celebrate for the first time ever in a big hotel. He agreed to pay for the Sofitel Hotel. All my friends were there – most were teachers as well – all my kids were there, his parents were there. Leila and her siblings were there. We were dancing all night when my friends started to ask where my husband was; it was already 10.30 pm. I was so happy, I did not mind my husband was not there yet.

My eldest kept ringing him, and when he answered, he said he was at a high school reunion. We decided to sing Happy Birthday without him. Jenny, my best friend, ordered a cake from Becky's Cake, with a photo of me in my flamenco dance costume with a red flower on the left side of my hair!

When Bruce arrived, everyone was coaxing him to dance with me, as there was a dance floor in the hotel function room. Let me preface what I'm about to say with the room being dark, only lit up by colourful disco strobe lights, so my friends never saw what happened next. When we were dancing, he pushed me away, and it jolted me in my brain! Wow! Really? You are pushing me away now even in public?

I kept that scene in my brain.

Looking back, the day I celebrated my 40th birthday was the birthday of his mistress, and she was just three weeks away from giving birth to their child. No wonder, he pushed me away that night.

Nightmares, Red Flags & a Car Accident

In 2016 I got a call from Immigration that I would have a hearing again for my permanent protection visa. My elder sister opened an online dating account for me. I had a few dates, but all were non-committal and just used me. I did not mind my elder sister helping me find someone, as she knew that I did not want to go back to my home country where I would relive the abuse of my ex-husband.

I thought of online dating and opened an account myself, where I met someone. He love-bombed me. He kept asking me out, but I told him to finish his divorce first. He kept coming to my door. He kept asking me to live with him, and five months later, I said yes. After a year together, he told me he would marry me.

He was nice to Arabella. She had her own room at his place, but so many times in the middle of the night Arabella would run to our bedroom, crying and screaming, and say she was scared. At times, she would just stand near me in our bedroom in the middle of the night, crying.

I thought this was the Australian partner I had been waiting for. We had fun times together. I cooked so many Filipino dishes he liked, such as adobo, sinigang, pochero, kare-kare and kaldereta. These are all famous Filipino soup-based dishes made with meat. We went on holidays together. He had his first ride in the airplane when we went to his mother in Dorrigo, near Coffs Harbour. We went to Canberra, Cockington Green Gardens and Questacon. He even joined me dancing with my friends at one point. I was glad that he always danced with me.

But it did not last long.

He went on a cruise to Vanuatu with his best mates in March 2017. He planned that before we met, and even if he would take me, I was not allowed to go out of Australian borders; Arabella and I had a protection visa clause that prohibited us from going out of Australia until we had our permanent protection residency.

When he arrived home, his phone kept ringing, and it was a girl. I gave him the phone. He said he met some girls there as friends. I said alright.

On my way to work at around 5.30 am the next day, I kept thinking about the fact that he was talking to another girl. I thought this was a red flag already. I felt sad that he was not the one I was looking for.

NIGHTMARES, RED FLAGS & A CAR ACCIDENT

I made a mistake again! While going down Wilson Road, towards Tahmoor, Wollondilly NSW, my steering wheel wiggled. I tried to hold it tight, but the car slowly flipped.

"Oh, no! God, please don't make me die yet. Not now, please! I need to take care of Bea. Please, Mama Mary, tell God not to make me die yet." I was screaming this over and over, praying while my Holden Adventra tumbled over, spinning me inside like I was in a washing machine!

I saw blood in my hand. I touched my face, my head. I touched the mirror and saw my face. Thank God, I didn't die! But I had to get out of here.

How do I get out? Where's my phone? I can't find my phone. Where are my Uggies?

I can't open the door! In a panic, I banged the door with my hands and feet to no avail. Thankfully, around five minutes or so, a Berrima bus passed by.

"Help! Help me!" I yelled out.

"It's alright; I'll help you." The bus driver approached and said to me.

"I can't open the door", I told him.

"Unlock the door", he patiently instructed.

I was too scared when the car flipped over, I didn't even realise the car door was still locked. I flicked up the lock, and the door slowly opened.

The bus driver pulled me out of my car and asked, "Can you walk?"

"Yes," I answered, standing up, but when I tried to walk, my hip felt so much pain and I was limping. The bus driver and another person on my side held me by the armpits to help me walk.

Two more cars stopped to help the bus driver.

"Just relax", they all said to me.

"Where is my phone? Where are my Ugg boots? I need to go to work," I said, disgruntled.

"You can't go to work. You just had a car accident", one of the people who helped me said.

I wish I knew the names of the other people who stopped so I could thank them, but I gave a letter of commendation to Berrima Bus lines to thank the driver who rescued me.

"Alright, I have to go now, as I need to bring my passengers to Picton train station. You have someone with you now", the bus driver assured me.

"Do you have a partner we can call?" the good Samaritan from Hilltop in Southern Highlands asked me.

"Yes," I said. "Can I go to work now?"

"No, you can't go to work. You have to go to the hospital. We will ring your work that you had a car accident, and we are waiting for the ambulance to bring you to the hospital."

NIGHTMARES, RED FLAGS & A CAR ACCIDENT

"OK", I sadly complied.

The ambulance came 40 minutes later, and I asked the responders to find my phone in my car. I thought my phone was my lifeline – well, up to now it is.

They finally got my phone and gave it to me while I was lying inside the ambulance.

I was brought to Liverpool Hospital, as they said I had a whiplash in my head and all head injuries go to Liverpool Hospital. I even remembered the date – it was in April 2017. I am not sure if it is the 27th or 17th though.

One thing I thank my Australian ex-partner for, though he abused me in the end, was that he visited me at the hospital and helped me to walk again by telling me that we were going dancing.

"We can take your neck brace now, as you are clear with head injury. No brain contusion, but you have a hairline hip fracture." The nurse explained.

"If you do not walk tonight, even to the toilet, your muscle will relax, and it will take a while for you to walk again. I suggest you walk tonight, even with how painful it is."

"It's painful, darling", I said to my Australian partner.

"No, darling. Come on, we're going dancing", he urged while lifting me slowly up from my bed. "We're dancing, dancing – come on, darling!" he kept saying while steadying me as I limped with so much pain – although, I was not fully focused on the pain, as I kept hearing the word *dancing, dancing*.

Now I know why I followed him in walking, even with so much pain – because dancing has always been my hidden therapy all my life.

Dancing always saved me at the end of the day.

"Good girl, baby girl, darling. Wow, you are here now!" I finally reached the toilet.

He did the same thing on my way back to my bed. This is the one thing I am grateful for, although in the end, he ended up still abusing me.

He was a good man, but the alcohol got the better of him. He drinks 10 to 11 beers a day, even during workdays. There was a time when I discreetly counted how many beers he drank. I put tally marks in the calendar, so I know that he really drinks a lot a day.

The nightmare now came to my brain that I was marrying the shadow of my alcoholic father. Arabella was having nightmares too. These nightmares had been going on since she was diagnosed with separation anxiety, as her elder sister and father always tried to get her from me.

When we were still in the Philippines, Bruce took Arabella one afternoon and took her to meet me at the petrol station. When Arabella saw me, she was crying, wanting to be with me. So, I went near the parked car as her father placed her on his lap. When I put my hand in to get Arabella, crying and her tiny hands and head

NIGHTMARES, RED FLAGS & A CAR ACCIDENT

reaching for me, Bruce started closing the car window! Arabella's head got stuck.

When I let go, he stopped pressing the window switch, then pressed it down slowly. Imagine torturing a child, slowly pinning her head in the car window.

Bruce then went and drove away, with Arabella on his lap.

Angered by his actions, I messaged him that it was not his visitation day, so if he took Arabella, I would call the police and say my daughter was kidnapped. When I came home, Arabella was back with her *yaya* (stay-in nanny).

The next day I had the courage to report the incident in Camp Karingal, the police district headquarters in Quezon City.

This was the reason Arabella always wanted to be with me at night. She was scared that her dad or her older sisters would take her away from me.

In 2014 she was also diagnosed with separation anxiety here in Australia. In one of her sessions with her psychologist, Michael Kirton, she drew a black monster who was trying to take her in the middle of the night.

Although my Australian ex-partner loved Arabella, he did not know how to discipline a child, as he never had one.

The intergenerational trauma of abuse that is ingrained in me just kept going. Unbelievable! I was seeing this as a clear pattern of an intergenerational trauma of abuse. One generation from my alcoholic father passed on to me, as my ex-husband abused me.

Then, I attracted the same pattern here in Australia, with an abusive man who was alcoholic and also verbally controlling. He was the combined shadow of my alcoholic father and my ex-husband's mental and verbal controlling abuse. He said the same things my ex-husband said.

"The police won't believe you if you leave me because you are not Australian." my Australian partner told me when I said, I am leaving as he said he wanted to be single.

I believe in the saying that the lessons will keep repeating until you get it. But I was not aware of what was happening to me, attracting all these abusive men since I was 15.

I prayed hard. Something had to be done. I kept praying that the government would help me with the best counsellors and psychologists that could help explain why I kept attracting all these abusive men.

I was helpless. The police helped me file the Apprehended Violence Order (AVO) in court, in which I had to appear at Bowral District Court.

"This is a constable police officer, Brenda. I wish to inform you that we are filing an AVO to your Australian partner, and it is not up to you. It is the law that allows us to protect women", a police officer rang me from Bowral Police Station.

NIGHTMARES, RED FLAGS & A CAR ACCIDENT

"I am scared. He might kill me and follow me, as he works here in Wollondilly", I said in fear.

"We are here to protect you. A lady police officer will be checking your welfare while we wait for the hearing of your AVO. In the meantime, there is an Interim AVO."

I thank the police officer who helped me that day when I had a panic attack after my Australian ex-partner trapped me, went in front of my car and told me with a pointed finger, "I'm gonna kill you. *Bang bang*!"

He sent me a text message, saying to leave his birth certificate since he was asleep. Before I left him, we were gathering documents, as he said he will sponsor me and marry me. I was the one who kept them in an envelope.

When I came to slip the envelope of his birth certificate, I was shocked to find him standing at the door, holding a beer. His face and eyes were all red. He had no shoes on. He was so drunk. I ran into my car and that's when he trapped me.

"You were the one who wanted to let go of me." I said, shivering. "I have to go." I was so scared but can't drive, as he was blocking my car after he went to the driver's side window.

As soon as he walked away, I drove but started crying hard. I was so scared that I ended up stopping at Balmoral, the suburb after Hilltop. I was crying and crying and rang the police. They came to me at Balmoral, where I parked near the fire station.

"I am so scared. He said he's gonna kill me!" I told them. "He might follow me." I was hiding and bending my leg as the police told me to get out of my car to talk about it.

I calmed down a bit, as I was assured by the police that they will help me be safe and that someone will ring me.

I had left his house and left in three days, as I asked Ben Boardman, the minister of Wilton Anglican Church, if he can find a place for me.

Thank God, the lovely Christian couple Heather and David from Douglas Park had a place for rent. A small one-bedroom granny flat in a nice dead-end property with a breathtaking cliff view. I called this heaven in my place where we stayed for two years.

This is my turning point. My anxiety got so heightened at this time.

I got approved for the Victim Services' program for victims of domestic violence. They helped me, and gave me extra hours of counselling. They also helped me buy furniture, basic household necessities such as TV, lounge, bed linens and towels. For this, I am very grateful.

My ex-husband's verbal abuse suddenly became untrue! He said the police won't believe me, but the police even helped me rebuild my life by filing an AVO.

My Australian ex-partner abused me and said the same thing – that I would end up in the street if I left him. He is an alcoholic, and it got the better of him.

NIGHTMARES, RED FLAGS & A CAR ACCIDENT

He told me he wanted to be single and go out, and then he would scream and shout at me, asking for money, which I don't have since I work only as a casual relief teacher.

All of Bruce's verbal abuse was ingrained in my system, as I started to unknowingly act out all the verbal abuse he told me, such as ending up poor and only renting. I walked and begged for food at Vinnies. I went from house to another house, not knowing that I was just projecting the mental torture ingrained to me by my ex-husband. I was helpless until the Department of Communities and Justice's Victim Services helped me and gave me extra hours of counselling.

I got better with healing the effects of intimidation by my ex-partner. But, up to now, some hidden abuse from my ex-husband is still going in my mind. Like Pandora's box, I need permanent protection, even here in Australia. The only thing that would stop him is for me to gain permanent protection with my daughter, Arabella.

Why is that? If Australian laws covered me for protection, he cannot do anything to kick me out of Australia.

Now I am free from him, from his control, from his abuse. Twenty-four years of manipulation, control and Stockholm syndrome domestic violence – that is what happened to me.

So! Did the verbal abuse from my ex-husband in 2015, where he said I was beautiful but no one loves me and no one likes to marry me still living in my system?

Who knows what life brings me now?

2019 - Rocky, the Unexpected Hero

I met Rocky while swimming at Douglas Park River at Wollondilly Shire, three days after my mum was buried. He came at the time my world fell apart – when my mother died.

Rocky is my hero! He is an 11-year-old boy, full of life and self-confidence.

He came near me and said, "Hi! You know what, we just went to this rock jump there," he pointed afar, "It's so awesome! You should try it with your daughter. My dad can take you. Tell my dad – the one in the green shirt. He'll take you there in a tinnie boat."

"I am pretty much a sports buff. I did rock climbing, had heaps of gold for sprint running, and I was a bronze medallist in swimming," I said with much confidence. "But haven't tried a rock jump."

Rocky shouted out to his dad, "Dad, can you take her and her daughter to the rock jump, please?"

"Alright, I'll take them after I finish this barbeque and we finish our lunch." Rocky's dad said while focusing on his barbeque, making sure it won't get burnt.

Once lunch was finished, Rocky said, "Dad, we can take them now to the rock jump." He proceeded to the tinnie and started to remove water from the boat.

"You know, my boat is slow. You might think it's a speedy one," Rocky's dad said. "I will take you and Rocky first because it's only three people per boat."

"How about my daughter and my niece?" I asked him.

"They'll go after us; I'll take them."

I jumped in the boat, then Rocky sat beside me, his dad in front of us. He started the engine … but it didn't sound good.

"Oh, no. The boat is not working."

I smiled. "No worries; there's next time."

"I'm sorry", he said, sheepish.

"All good", I said with a smile

I jumped off the boat and swam. He followed and had a chat with me while I was relaxing in the water. "I have been single for

2019 – ROCKY, THE UNEXPECTED HERO

nine years, and I just focus on my boy. I go to work, and my mum takes him to school – much easier for me for work, as my mum looks after him while I am at work", he shared.

"Me too. I am a single mum just focusing on my daughter. She has Physie after school, King's Kids on Thursdays at church," I told him.

"Wow! Full on, aye?" he said, impressed.

A few minutes passed by. "I'll try to fix the boat now", he announced.

Vrroomm! The tinnie roared back to life.

"What did you do?" This time it's my turn to be impressed.

"Nothing. I just let it rest a bit, then it worked."

I was looking at the nice gorge with the rocks kissing in between, the dried leaves and soothing cool water in the river, when Rocky said, "You know, my dad can take you for a fourbie drive or a ride in his Seny."

"Oh, what's a Seny?"

"It's my car, a Holden Senator", the dad of Rocky said.

"Oh, OK." I was smiling a bit. Wow, this son was selling his dad to me like he is the best dad in the world!

While Rocky was talking, I was looking at his dad, and my mind was saying, *Oh no, Bren. You can't fall in love. You might make a mistake again.*

Why am I in this when I am supposed to mourn the loss of my mum?

"Oh, my dad can call you. Give your number to my dad", Rocky said, then paused. "Oh, hang on. My dad has no phone," he thought aloud, forehead slightly frowning like it's the biggest problem in the world.

"It's OK, Rocky," his dad interjected, chuckling. "I can call her on the landline at home."

I just smiled, so amazed with this outspoken, friendly, confident and gutsy 11-year-old boy!

We arrived at the rock. The leaves and trees were all brown! It was too hot; even the dry trees seemed dead from the heat of the sun.

I was tippy-toeing! Walking in my cozzie (bathing costume) felt good. My feet burned while walking towards our rock jump saga that Rocky had motivated me to go to.

We arrived at the top of the Douglas Park Gorge.

"That is too high for me to go down a steep rock!" I exclaimed.

2019 – ROCKY, THE UNEXPECTED HERO

"Don't worry, I'll help you. Here, step on my hand", Rocky's dad gladly helped me down the steep end of the rock.

"Wow, it's so beautiful here on top of the rock! It's my first time here, and I live here."

I exclaimed as I saw the picturesque scene of the green trees at the Douglas Park gorge river from the top, with the rocks kissing the water in between.

"You're here now. You're committed now. You can't go back", Rocky's dad said.

"Just keep your head up high, keep your body straight. Don't move, just do it." he instructed regarding the jump.

"I can't. I am too scared", I told him.

"Alright, I'll jump first, then you. Make sure you commit, alright?"

I was keen to do it to remove my past hurts.

"If something happens to me, will you look after me down there?" I asked Rocky's dad, who is already 20 metres below.

"Oh, yeah. After 10 minutes, I'll come and get you," he said with a chuckle.

"I'm joking, I'll look after you."

They waited for me to jump in the water for ages with much patience. Thoughts were swimming in my head. *If I die here of a heart attack, what about my daughter, Bea? Who cares? I don't think I'll die. They've been doing this. I'll try it not for them, but for myself.*

Finally, I closed my eyes, let go, let God.

"Mum, I love you so much. I know you will be with me forever, looking from the sky",

I silently uttered, talking to my mum.

Closed eyes!

Deep breath!

Heart thumping.

Clenched teeth.

I held my breath.

"God help me. Be with me. This is for you, Mum."

Jump!

While in the air, eyes closed, my two legs curled up like a baby and my head bowed down in fear!

As soon as I was submerged in water, a deep feeling of nostalgia came to me – an awesome renewed feeling I felt deep in the water after that fearful jump.

2019 – ROCKY, THE UNEXPECTED HERO

Rocky did get my number, but his dad followed me on my way to my car as I packed up our mats, hats and sunscreen.

"Mum, it's too hot!" I saw Arabella tippy-toeing.

Hearing this, Rocky's dad grabbed her by her arm and carried her to the car.

"Can I have your number again? Rocky might have lost it", he asked once he has placed Arabella inside.

After I gave him my number, he said softly, "Alright, I'll give you a buzz. See you later."

As I walked to my car, my niece teased, "*Oi, Tita* (Auntie) Bren, how about that? He got your number. He might be the one, *Tita*."

"I know," I said, smiling. "We'll see. He might not ring, who knows." I added, not getting my hopes up.

I drove my niece and her daughter to the train station on their way to the airport to Melbourne, where they live, as she just attended the funeral of her grandma, my mum.

Run to Paradise (Uluru) on my 52nd Birthday

Million Dollar Memories with Arabella

Dear Mum,

Happy birthday!

I hope you have an amazing day and all your wishes come true. I hope when you read this book you will enjoy it and inspire you to create a page-turning book!

I know that the book you create will be sensational because your story is truly touching! You survived many years of abuse and built an amazing life, and in doing so, you saved me.

There is no way I can describe how thankful I am to you for saving me and bringing me to Australia. You are a strong, kind, loving, bubbly amazing woman. Thank you so much for everything you do for me!

I hope you are very happy and that your life will be filled with joy!

Because you deserve it all – a good, loving husband, an amazing career and your permanent residence!!! You are an amazing, beautiful woman, and you may be 52, but you look 30!!! Lally (Grandma) is smiling down at us and is so proud and happy of who you are.

Your book will inspire and touch others who have survived domestic violence or people who are going through it and encourage them to keep going.

You truly are a super woman – you escaped from a toxic, abusive relationship and came to Australia with absolutely nothing but a bit of cash, which isn't even close to what you deserve!!!

Without money, you built and worked your way up to become a teacher and have an amazing life. You fought and worked so hard for everything you have, and I aspire to be just like you! But in my wildest dreams, I couldn't be half as brave and strong as you.

Queen Elizabeth may have been the queen of the world, but you are the QUEEN OF MY WORLD!

RUN TO PARADISE (ULURU) ON MY 52ND BIRTHDAY

I hope that your birthday and our week at Uluru brings you joy and creates unforgettable memories!

You deserve all the happiness in the universe!

You're the best mum in the whole universe!

Love,
Bea

I cried while reading Arabella's birthday letter for me, written in a biography book about Queen Elizabeth. We even shared to buy this book, as she only had $12 in cash, and I had to pay half of it so she could buy me a birthday gift.

The thoughtfulness of Arabella is enough for me to say that I really made the best decision to rebuild our life here in Australia and save her from further abuse and being used by her father. I saved her from being a potentially disrespectful and materialistic daughter, and she grew up into a loving, sensible and caring daughter.

A new horizon for me. Uluru gave me the reason, I thought as I posed for the first time in Uluru, a paradise I call it now. I am in the lucky country. I believe in the saying that Australia is a lucky, beautiful country.

Welcome to the Country!

"We pay respect to the First Nations Australian people of this sacred land, Uluru", I whispered as I knelt down and touched the red rock sand.

I was lucky enough to save money for my birthday in January 2023.

"Thanks for this Uluru trip, Mum." Bea thanked me every single day in the four days we were there.

"This is paradise!" I exclaimed while looking at the red lands of Uluru.

RUN TO PARADISE (ULURU) ON MY 52ND BIRTHDAY

I fell in love with Uluru the moment I saw the red rocks. The heat that was gushing in me felt like a new feeling of healing. As I saw the hotel with the view of red rocks and white, neat, well-pressed bed linens with exotic Aboriginal-designed throw pillows, I felt so pampered! I felt so blessed. So serene. I took so many photos and posted so many reels on social media. Now I always look back at the million-dollar memories that Arabella and I made.

This is me – vibrant, always optimistic and loving life. I call this my heaven in paradise. Uluru is my heaven in paradise, and so is Australia! Australia is the most beautiful, welcoming country in the world! The most welcoming multicultural country in the world! There is so much more to say – it's a lucky country that has a unique Australian value of mateship where help is on the way, freedom, respect and equal opportunity.

Thank you for giving me my second life, Australia!

Gilee Cried Abuse!

I had to save Gilee back in the Philippines, as she was suffering the same control and manipulation that her father did to me. Fortunately, while I was talking to her, I was in the middle of a counselling session with my counsellor from STARTTS (NSW Service for the Treatment and Rehabilitation of Torture and Trauma Survivors).

Upon hearing Gilee's cry for help, I broke down into tears during our session and had to get water from the fridge, as I could not breathe. I was hyperventilating. My head hurt so much, and I felt like throwing up. My counsellor was so good in calming me down and making me feel lighter.

All the things I had suffered from my ex-husband, Gilee was unfortunately suffering too – all the control, intimidation, manipulation, mental and psychological abuse and isolation. This is totally what is happening to Gilee now. She had to say sorry to her Dad after the video of abuse in 7 November 2023 happened.

She once again lost her patience and pushed me to send her money even if I do not have extra yet.

From 2019 to 2022, she would ask for help but would eventually go back to the cycle of domestic violence. Her dad and her siblings would get her back easily, as she was so weak with all the medicine her father gave her through a psychiatrist. In 2022 she asked me for help, then after less than a month, she told me that she would stay there because she would miss her niece and nephew.

Gilee spoke to Bea as well and convinced her to forgive her father, saying "He is still your father," and "He gave you gifts," and "Who paid your Sydney BridgeClimb for you before?".

"How can I forgive someone who does not even recognise me, doesn't provide for me here, and abused me? He tried to choke me with the car window." Bea answered through my Facebook Messenger account.

Allow me to share the precious story of my dear fourth daughter, Gileena, or Bella. With her permission, I am sharing her story, which she sent in Messenger last June 2023: (Trigger warning: suicide attempts, foul language)

> Thank you for your advice. I am currently taking Depakote (anticonvulsant medication), Jovia (escitalopram), Sertraline (antidepressant medication) and Rivotril (benzodiazepine) as needed. I also have PCOS (polycystic ovary syndrome) and took Duphaston (progestin medication) to have my period.

GILEE CRIED ABUSE!

My family is frustrated with me not sleeping properly, but I can't sleep because I think of how they treat me. There was a time I felt so traumatised before sleeping; I shivered while laying down on my side, eyes open. I was scared that my dad would open the door and check my room; the whole family has no concept of privacy and boundaries. I would remember the harmful, violent thing he did to me every time someone knocks on my door.

When I was in 3rd year high school, I wanted to leave because I was devastated with bullies, heartbreak, the way my family treated me, and my mom leaving. I felt abandoned, so I packed my things and argued with my dad, and when things got heated, I locked myself in the bathroom and cried nonstop, wanting to disappear. He banged the door and kicked it too. It was the scariest moment of my life. The mark on the door was painted on after a few years, and it felt like a bullet hole was treated with a bandaid.

My dad would shout at me as a kid and tell me, "*Siraulo kang bata kang tanga!*" ("You crazy, stupid kid!") as he held my face, punch me lightly and pinch me in the legs.

He told the nanny to open the door with scissors. The nanny had left when it all happened, so there was no witness – all there was violence and a kid crying out for help from fear of her father.

Please, if something happens, help me. I have no idea what to do. He complains and dictates what I should do all the time; so does the rest. I feel like I am trapped and controlled. I contemplated giving up and just jumping over the Tumana Bridge beside our house in Marikina.

Today I called my mom to see how she was doing. I haven't seen her in person for nine long years. In those nine long years, I had the worst experience with my family from my dad's side because I committed suicide countless times. I overdosed on the medicine I used for my medical condition and drank liquor around April.

My doctor currently has my phone, according to my dad. I don't have a way to use a phone with a sim card, and I feel so trapped and controlled. I was never free to be me. As a person from the LGBTQIA+, all I want to hear from them is that they love me and will treat me better because I do not deserve this. They are okay with me being bisexual, but who knows what they will do next to lie and manipulate me.

I am not the weakest link. In fact, I am the strongest, and they had no idea that I had a plan to move out if I had the money. They are overprotective to the point that I feel like I'm clinging on to them. I cried and broke down while talking to my uncle from Australia, and my mom listened to my complaints as well.

I feel like it's too late for me to see Mum and my sister, as well as the rest of my relatives in Australia. I was so excited to visit my grandma, Lally, but she passed away, and I never got to see her. I really wish Lally will guide and help me get out of this nightmare.

GILEE CRIED ABUSE!

My dream was to hug my mom and sister again, even for the last time. I wanted to visit her and all, but fate was never on our side. I argued with my eldest sister, and after that, I hid in my room and hung myself with a jump rope and choked myself, hoping to disappear and finally be able to rest from what I am feeling.

I committed suicide for the second time this June and felt frustrated because my dad cut the jump rope using the scissors our maid gave and asked the maid to throw it away. I feel like I have no choice. I can't do anything, and they tell me I can't go out because I should be with my family when all I did was pour out all my love and effort to them. I feel so empty; they emptied me. I feel drained and stressed, and if I stay here longer, I might end up jumping over a bridge.

They mock me and laugh at me all the time, telling me that I won't make it to Australia. They also told me that my mum might make me her maid, and I won't survive. But I want to feel free and assured. I really wish Australia would consider protecting me from this pain I am feeling. They don't think I am respectable, and they don't believe in me. All I want is someone to love me the way I should be loved and to be appreciated. I hope and pray that I will be with my family in Australia soon. I also want to watch the Taylor Swift concert in Australia with my mum and sister so that I will feel better. I wish that I could be in Australia, or at least visit someday.

Gileena Hernandez

Please help me pray to God that Gilee gets a visa for Australia. I pray to the Divine God to intervene and save Gilee.

As of 23 October 2023, Gilee was doing well. I checked on her every day through Facebook Messenger. She has followed my advice not to drink her medicines. I noticed the difference; she was bubblier and more relaxed. When I used to talk to her before, she looked like she was drugged up, which is not so normal.

I knew there was nothing wrong with her. Gilee has learned to assert herself to her father, but she still gets verbally and mentally abused.

Bruce asked her how she was without the medicine.

"Dad, I am fine."

"Good." Bruce told Gilee.

"He was only happy that I am not taking medicine because it is expensive; it's all about money to him, Mum", Gilee told me.

"Gilee, I am so happy for you and proud of you for sticking up for yourself. Keep on going. I am your cheerleader", I told her.

I have long prayed for this moment – that Gilee would at least be free from medication. I knew deeply in my heart that she was not mentally sick. Although, she may have mental health issues, that is because her father is throwing out in her system and her dad does not know how to raise her.

GILEE CRIED ABUSE!

"Mum, they're going to give me an injection because they said I will get sick", Gilee once called me via Messenger, crying in fear.

"Don't worry, Gilee, I will tell your big sister not to do that to you", I assured her. "Lock your door."

I've had enough! I messaged my eldest daughter on 27 September 2023 via Messenger and she said, "Yes, no injection for Gilee."

Hurray, Mum Brenda! my mind shouted out. I actually am so happy defending Gilee over Messenger.

I see the red flags quickly now. They wanted to give Gilee an injection to put her to sleep all day and night, like what happened before, because she had been chatting with me about her abuse. Her big sister and her father were making her sleep an issue so that she could be back to sleeping all day and night, drugged up! Unbelievable!

That never stopped there. As told by Gilee, now that she has cried abuse, all the more they have deprived her of money and basic needs, like clothing. She needed money to go to her singing engagements.

"Please tell Gilee not to have too many commitments because she demands transportation and meals for her non-paying jobs. She texts me to book her a Grab", her big sister complained to me.

"Her father abused her," I asserted again. "He has to leave Gilee alone. And he has to give her an allowance. I will expose the abuse if you do not give Gilee allowance."

This is it. In real life situation, I am actually experiencing an ongoing domestic violence abuse I suffered, but it was in the person of my poor daughter, Gilee.

This time, it was my eldest daughter involved, as I had never talked to my ex-husband since 2015, when he said over the phone, "'*Di ako magpapadala ng $100,000. Wala akong pera. Maganda ka nga, wala namang may gustong magpakasal sa'yo.*" ("I am not sending the $100,000. I don't have money. You may be beautiful, but no one wants to marry you.")

He said that in our native language, as he barely speaks English. I taught all my children how to speak English.

I had to be tough on my eldest daughter. I have to cut this intergenerational trauma pattern of abuse that has been passed on to us – to my family and to my family of origin.

My daughter understood me now. I knew my silence would speak to her, that I meant business. All I wanted was for Gilee to be out of her father's control, manipulation and intimidation while waiting to get her Australian visa.

So, I had to say my piece to my eldest daughter over Messenger. "I was in Gilee's situation, so I understand her. I have compassion for her. Mine was worse, I was in so much marital distress. Your dad was able to convince me to get a property title and live in a condo with a one-year rental, but Bea won't be there!

GILEE CRIED ABUSE!

"And do you remember when I woke up from my marital distress on my birthday? I cried and came back. It was never my decision to be kicked out of my own house.

That was my past. I will remember the lesson forever. I will never forget what happened to me there.

"I can see Gilee suffering as much as I did when I was there. You even told me, 'Mum, stay in your condo. *Dun ka na sa* condo *mo. Dito lang si* Bea.' ('Mum, stay in your condo. Just stay there. Bea will stay here.'). I was crying. Benedict was on the floor, kneeling towards me, holding my hand, and he told you, 'Geo, Mum can stay here. It's her birthday.'"

"I am teary eyed now. Gilee feels the same thing as me. She wants to get out of that abusive dad of hers. I don't have any grudge towards you or Ann 11.

You are adults, and you can choose what you like to do in your life. But I will forever be grateful for the life lessons that God has given this experience I had with you."

Take a guess whether I received any replies.

Nothing. I did not receive a single reply.

From the time I left my marriage, my children had been told by their dad that they would lose their inheritance if they took their mother's side.

I was just wondering; the battle is finished! I am out of their abusive cycle.

But still, their father continually abuses Gilee.

I am frustrated with how my eldest daughter came to this intergenerational trauma of control and manipulative abuse.

I know that one day she will see the light too. I won't stop connecting with her.

I won't stop making her realise that Gilee is fine and nothing is wrong with her.

Gilee told me once over our video call, "Maybe Geo has trauma bonding with me." She is slowly realising it now. Gilee has come so far; although, I know she would need a lot of counselling and therapy.

Now that she has cried abuse, Gilee keeps me updated with what is happening there at present as of writing this book.

Karma is a God!

"Mum, Dad had karma", Gilee said in our video call. "Linda (former housemaid) was asking for ₱200,000 before she and her family agree to evacuate the unit at one of our properties where Dad told them to live."

At present, Linda, a former housemaid whom my ex-husband allowed to stay in one of his properties with her seven children and partner wouldn't leave unless she gets money.

Back then, my ex-husband kept defending Linda when my kids were little until they were teenagers. He kept saying that Linda was a lot better than my children.

GILEE CRIED ABUSE!

Yep, you never get away with the consequences of what you have done.

Everything here on earth is never in vain! Sorry, his own abuse with us bit him in the ass after more than 20 years. I was calm when I heard it.

She also told me that her grandmother is transferring property titles under my children's names to take me out of the property (it is still in my name and my ex-husband's name).

This is my wish for Gilee: I wish that she comes here and rebuild her life like me. I wish she finds her happiness in this lucky, beautiful country of Australia. I wish for the Australian government to give her a chance to have a visa. I wish one day I could hug her tight and make her safe here.

I wish I can say to her, "Gilee we are here in Australia with Lally now", just as I did with Arabella.

I love you, Gilee, with all my heart. Hang in there. You will make it.

My dear daughter, Gilee, attempted suicide several times, as mentioned. Her father did not even bring her to the emergency department to treat her overdose.

Gilee told me that they were all laughing and mocking her for being groggy and drugged. How cruel!

I am sorry, Gilee, this happened to you, yet your siblings even laughed and mocked you. I want to tell you that they love you too; they just don't know any better.

This is the effect of the intergenerational trauma pattern – they don't know how to react, so they copy their father.

This 7 December 2023, Gilee started talking back to me again. Sadly, I just found out she lives with her grandmother again in the heritage house where we used to stay.

I started to think that I can tell Gilee to let her grandmother help her get a visa to visit me. I thought of paying it forward, let my mother-in-law have her own retribution by helping Gilee come here in Australia. I thought about it to cut the patterns of intergenerational trauma of abuse of control.

As of this writing, December 2023, Gilee said her grandmother will help her get a tourist visa. I am praying hard that Gilee, whom I have not seen for nearly 10 years.

In the same breath, I have boundaries now on how to protect me, Arabella and Gilee from her grandmother who is also controlling and manipulative.

Sadly, last 22 December 2023, Gilee tried to hurt herself again. She scratched a knife on her stomach and said that she hopes her stomach will be smaller.

She had so much mental stress and trauma, that she was not able to cope since the incident of abuse last 7 November 2023 when she tried to record the abuse of her dad and he physically and verbally abused her. He strangled, punched, kicked, pinched, slapped her, and when he tried to run away outside, her dad pushed her on the gate while strangling her.

After that incident, she had no economic support from her father. Her eldest sister would give her money, but not regularly. Then she met a guy from TikTok she was chatting with, whom she never met. He has been love-bombing her.

He said that he loves her and that he has a lot of savings, so he can make her stay in their suburban Cagayan Valley.

Oh, a weird thing he said to Gilee was that he has one year to live, so he would go to California in March to have a heart surgery. Then he would take Gilee and pay for her plane ticket.

This was just on top of what Gilee has been suffering from being isolated with all the family, relatives and her cousins.

She was not even allowed to attend the wedding of her sister last December 2023 because her father is there. But her sister, Ann 111, gladly scheduled a photo shoot so they could wear their gowns and re-enact the wedding photos.

It was a good riddance, though, this was so heartbreaking for me.

I cried on my own, thinking about Gilee that she had a mental breakdown again.

The good riddance is her eldest sister now is looking after her, her brother as well, and visiting her at the mental hospital facility.

She had to spend Christmas and New Year there, although she was already alright after Christmas according to the psychiatrist. But her father told my eldest daughter that Gilee had to stay till she comes after her holidays from Korea, as he could not handle Gilee and does not talk to the doctor anymore (I hope so). It is my eldest daughter now.

"You're a soldier", my only son told her eldest sister as they coaxed each other who would tell me (mum) about Gilee,

My eldest daughter told me the sad story. I cried on the phone while talking to her because she hurt herself again and it was ingrained abuse.

It was like her father is slowly killing her. She has to be with me. My eldest daughter is looking after Gilee now, and I made sure the medicine will still make her function and not sleep day and night.

At present, Gilee's psychiatrist gave her all the medicine back for bipolar disorder. But these are all the same with her symptoms of complex PTSD from long years of physical, emotional, mental abuse.

I really have to save Gilee here.

She will be stuck there with what her father ingrained in her that her mental illness is because of her bipolar disorder and not connected to domestic violence.

This research below will prove that Gilee has complex post-traumatic stress disorder when she tried to hurt herself again last 22 December 2023.

She was hopeless because her father was economically abusing her, so she had no choice but to take revenge through messaging me about her perpetrator with her dad. She messaged me that she wanted to take over the business of her dad since he is injured.

Here are the symptoms of CPTSD, I got from this CPTSD Foundation research:

https://cptsdfoundation.org/2020/11/23/misdiagnosis-is-it-bipolar-disorder-or-complex-post-traumatic-stress-disorder/

Her symptoms of complex post-traumatic stress disorder include:

- Losing or reliving memories of traumatic events
- Difficulty regulating mood
- Rage
- Sudden mood swings
- Depression
- Suicidal thoughts or actions
- Feeling detached from oneself
- Feeling ashamed
- Feeling guilty
- Difficulty trusting others
- Feeling different from others
- Becoming obsessed with revenge for the perpetrator
- Difficulty maintaining relationships
- Seeking or becoming a rescuer
- Being hyperalert
- Feeling a loss of spiritual attachment
- Depending on religion for self-worth

Gileena acted these out last 22 December 2023 and told her big sister that she needed to be confined in the hospital, as she was cutting her stomach with a knife to remove her fat. Her online boyfriend broke up with her because he said his ex-girlfriend is pregnant.

Combined with the years of her abuse of control and manipulation from her father, Gilee did not take this very well. This is the reason she had a mental breakdown again.

Right now she is still in Metro Psyche Mental Facility. The psychiatrist said she is really getting better and can be discharged.

As of this writing, in January 2024, Gilee just got out of mental facility hospital after staying for more than three weeks,

The intergenerational trauma patterns of control through my eldest daughter Ann 1 was cut!

"Hallelujah!"

She is supporting me and Gilee now in any way she can.

Thank heavens for this! Thank you, Ann 1, for being the best eldest daughter and for looking after Gilee too!

My million-dollar wishes for my adult children:

These will be my wishes to all my other daughters:

To my two eldest daughters, I am sorry that you have to deal with this intergenerational trauma that was passed on to us. I wish you could come here with your family this time so I can cuddle my first grandson, Jake.

I want you to know that you are all welcome here in Australia, so I can see my grandchildren and hug you as your mother. I gave birth to both of you.

I know you by heart. We had good times when you were kids. I wish we could all be here in Australia, for you to see Mum happy and back to doing what she loves – teaching.

Thank you, Ann 1, for your message, that you never bought into your dad's belief that you would not respect me when you grow as an adult.

I am still waiting for Ann 11 to talk to me, but it's OK. I know one day she will, especially since she is in New Zealand with her family now. I wish her all the best of luck there.

Of course, to my kindest, level-headed third daughter, Ann 111, who is now in America and living happily with her fiancé in the United States of America, thank you for visiting Mum and introducing me to your fiancé, Jaime.

How respected I felt when you came here.

Thank you for always respecting me. Never even once did you disrespect me, and only cried to me because your dad said you would lose all the inheritance if I got all my property share settlement in the marriage.

Remember when I gathered all of you and said, "Mum is still alive. No one will lose inheritance here."? I knew, as a mum, the reason you were crying was because you did not want to say that to me, but you were pressured to say it because your dad told you to.

I am sorry about all these, ANN 111. All is well now.

Mum has rebuilt her life here in Australia. I am sorry that you had to go through all this.

I wish you all great things in your future married life.

I am sorry that I cannot attend your wedding in the Philippines. I have died there.

I do not want to remember any of my past there. Who knows, if I have a good, honourable, respectable Australian partner, then I could go to your American wedding venue in May 2024.

This is just my wish, though. Whether it will come true or not doesn't matter because my love for you is enough for you to live and share. I am always in your heart, Ann 111, and you are always in my heart.

To all my six beautiful children, touch your heart. Mum is inside your heart. No matter what happens, Mum loves you and will forever be here for you to protect you as I did when you were all kids.

An open letter to my dear, beautiful, loving son

Dearest son Benedict,

Thank you for loving Mum more than I can imagine. I am in tears right now writing this letter for you.

You don't know how much I am so filled with love for you when you held my hand and knelt on my bed and told your eldest sister, "Geo, Mum is crying. Mum can stay here; it's her birthday today."

That moment made me say that I really have to go, as you see that I am being controlled by my own eldest daughter.

I wanted to show to you that is not on. So, I grappled to make sure I walk away with Bea, as I do not want you, Bea and Gilee to see me being abused by my two adult daughters. And it is not their fault, son. They are all victims of the intergenerational trauma of abusive pattern that has passed on our family.

Yes, son, we have cut the intergenerational trauma.

Yes son, I am crying, sobbing in tears now, here in my lounge, wiping my tears that fell on my neck. But these tears are tears of healing as I realise now that you are a young man, 22 years old.

You never changed your kind, caring, nice, fine, loving character. From the time I left you when I had to go when you were 12, I knew you would be fine. I knew you would stick up for yourself. I knew you would have my heart. I knew you would have my loving and pure soul. I was right.

Thank you, son, for everything that you have shown to me.

The love and the faith you have for me as your mother is enough to tell me that I have indeed cut the intergenerational trauma pattern of abuse in the family, as you stayed loving, caring and kind to me, your siblings and the people around you.

I remember our video call when you told me, "Mum, I don't blame you for leaving Dad for what he has done to you."

I remember again when you knelt on my bed. "Mum, please stay. I want you to drive me and my friends to my basketball games, my parties. Please, Mum, I want you to stay and drive me to school."

"No, son, this is not my home now. I am sorry I can't stay. I have to go back to my home, Australia."

AN OPEN LETTER TO MY DEAR, BEAUTIFUL, LOVING SON

I am still in tears remembering this, as I did not tell you and show you before that it broke my heart to say no to you. But the rest was history now.

This is my empowered self now saying I made the right decision. Nothing happens by accident for us and our family. We are meant to be where we are now, son.

Look at how loving, caring and kind you are. I raised you for 12 years. I drove you to your soccer games when I enrolled you and Gilee at the Ateneo football clinic when you were 5 years old. I drove you to your preparatory exam review, if not Red, the driver, just so you would pass the Ateneo kindergarten exam. I drove you and joined you in watching the Ateneo UAAP Games. I drove you to your eye doctor for your lazy eyes.

"Mum, look at that Healing Mass by Fr Corsie Legaspi. Can that priest heal me? Can he heal my lazy eyes so I won't have to wear an eye patch or this thick eyeglasses?" I was so happy hearing your faith in God, even as a young boy.

"Mum, why is God god?" Oh my God, son, you asked that question to me while we were listening at Ateneo's First Communion seminar.

"Why don't you go to the priest after and ask him that question?" I answered.

"Father," you asked the priest presiding the seminar. "Why is God god?" my beautiful son asked the priest after our first communion seminar for parents.

The priest laughed and said, "Oh, that is a very philosophical question. What's your name?"

"Benedict", you answered.

Son, from the time you were in my womb, I prayed hard to St Benedict and St Scholastica. All the Missionary Benedictine Sisters of Tutzing Philippines from St Scholatica's College Manila, where I used to teach, prayed for me to have a baby boy.

I chose 15 August 2001 to give birth to you. It is the Feast of the Assumption of Mother Mary.

Thank you, son, for always heeding God's call. Thank you for being a man of God, who follows him and his word.

I just wish you would visit me here one day in Australia with your friends. I am always thinking and praying for you. Not a day passes by that I did not think of you and pray for you.

I love you, Joshy, my only son.

Your loving, sweet Mum

AN OPEN LETTER TO MY DEAR, BEAUTIFUL, LOVING SON

Begging the God of Australia, hear my plea

It was too hard to walk away, as he always tried to get the kids away from me. The first time I try to walk away, my mother-in-law took my two small kids.

After that, it stuck on my mind that if I leave him, they would do the same thing – take away all my kids from me.

I stayed abused to protect my kids from being taken away from me and losing them, which I cannot afford to happen. It took me a long time to step back, as in the beginning I did not realise that what he was doing was abuse.

I was in stuck in the cyclical dilemma of surviving and hiding my abuse.

I was too young in the marriage. I thought it was a normal thing.

His coercive controlling abuse would go from hiding car keys, turning off the lights, humiliating me in front of my children, that in the end I realised my children will not respect me anymore because I stayed in the abuse and they saw me not doing anything.

I grappled to walk away when my nerves were already shaking in 2011 and I could not stop crying, so this was my signal to walk away and take Arabella with me.

I was right, as the psychotherapist Inge Rosario warned me when I told my history of 24 years of controlling abuse.

She told me, "I warn you, your adult kids will end up abusing you because you stayed in this kind of abuse."

I pleaded for protection in Australia, so Arabella would not end up like her other elder sisters who ended up abusing their own mother.

I still fear that Arabella would be taken away from me here and we'd be sent back.

I still experience poor mental health as a result of this abuse. I suffer from post-traumatic stress disorder and hypervigilance that my ex-husband is still prying on me here in Australia to put trouble on me and take Arabella from me.

I am already in Australia, a safe country, but it is hard to cope with even in a safe place with lots of support, including mental health support.

BEGGING THE GOD OF AUSTRALIA, HEAR MY PLEA

As the mental trauma I suffered is so deep and extremely affected my way of life,

I cannot even go and have a wish to have a boyfriend, as I am scared that they might end up abusing me like my ex-husband.

My current mental health treatment is counselling every second Thursday with Amy of STARTTS and my GP gave me a higher dose of Sertraline of 50 mg, as my present medication.

I used to have 25 mg Sertraline but could not sleep and had nightmares, nausea and severe headache during this preparation of this hearing, so I had to ring my GP to help me with my sleepless nights because of reliving and remembering all my mental trauma.

I see my GP once a month or whenever I feel the mental triggers of my trauma, like sleepless nights, nightmares, nausea, vomiting and headache.

If I am sent back I will not be able to access this mental health support, as I could not afford it with no financial means, and my ex-husband for sure will just lock me up in a mental facility if I asked for mental health medicine.

He thinks of a misjudgement of mental health stigma that people who suffer anxiety and depression are crazy without a future, just like what he said to Gilee that the ambulance was waiting and that she was fat and no one would hire her.

I have rebuilt my life here in Australia and have become an esteemed public school teacher and casual Catholic school teacher.

This is my home now, and my connection with the Wollondilly community, my friends and my church are already grounded with so much welcoming spirit here.

If I am sent back to the Philippines, I feel I am dead there and it will be totally different, as it will trigger all my mental trauma.

It is not the place; it is ingrained in my mental health issues with PTSD and hypervigilance.

My students love the way I teach, as I do it with so much fun and engagement by singing and dancing for them if they finish their work.

I would not be able to do these things if I am sent back.

I will definitely have a mental nervous breakdown and extreme fear that will cause me to have panic attacks and severe PTSD, and I will not function as productively as I do here.

I even fear for my life there, as I know my ex-husband will continue to abuse me and my children.

I do not even see and talk to my ex-husband now, but I still feel the mental trauma and triggers of panic attack whenever I think about all my abuse from him.

My fears if I return to the Philippines

My greatest fear if I am to return to the Philippines is that Arabella and I will be separated.

The significant fear that what happened to Gileena will definitely happen to me and Arabella.

I worry that the continuing coercive control domestic abuse of my ex-husband to Gileena by strangling, kicking, pinching and pushing her on the gate when she tried to escape will happen to me and Arabella.

He already had records of several physical abuse on me.

He pushed me before and twisted my arms while I was carrying Arabella because I got the photocopy of the property titles.

Arabella is so young, and I don't think she will survive there as much as I did, as I was older.

The abusive behaviour of my ex-husband still continues, with Gileena sharing all the stories with me, and it is being committed against Gileena's rights.

Now she has mentally suffered a lot because of it, and I am afraid this is what I will face again if returned with Arabella.

The continuing coercive control and manipulation domestic abuse of my ex-husband is pathological, as said by Dr Ronquillo, the psychiatrist I consulted in 2011 when I left my abusive marriage.

Dra. Ronqullo said that my ex-husband will get worse, as he has controlling and manipulative disorder, using another object to abuse me, not only physically. She said to walk away as far as I can, as he will use people to pry on me.

This is evidently true, as he continued to abuse Gileena, and he will definitely haunt me with the release of my memoir, which was not intentional to cause him trouble.

But because of his controlling disorder he will hire someone to lock me up, and I will never see my daughter.

This happened to Gileena. She was locked up at mental facility in and out from 2015–2018. I was not able to speak to her. It was only in 2018 when she started to communicate with me again.

His controlling abuse will significantly hurt me and Arabella, and we will not survive. Gileena committed suicide several times from his abuse, which she could not take anymore.

I fear that Arabella might do the same thing, and I as her mother would be devastated if it happens to Arabella.

She is too young to be subjected to the torture and control of her father. No mother would allow that to happen.

If I am sent back, the mental health impact on me would be so severe, that I will not survive anymore.

Even the thought of being sent back already triggers all the mental trauma now. What more if it happens in real life?

I was suicidal in 2018, then I had so much counselling and therapy with experts in attachments of toxic relationship and STARTTS expert in mental trauma and torture. Now I function really well and am an esteemed casual high school teacher at a local school where I live.

BEGGING THE GOD OF AUSTRALIA, HEAR MY PLEA

My thoughts of coming back will give me a severe mental nervous breakdown. Mental nervous breakdown runs in my family.

I saw my other two big sisters having mental nervous breakdown, and they had to stay in a mental facility.

The mental healthcare in the Philippines is so limited, that they even have two psychiatrists for whole three big islands of the Philippines.

I mentioned this in my previous research of DFAT COUNTRY 2020.

I will not be able to afford a private psychiatrist and counselling, as the private mental health is too expensive and my continued healing here will just be back to square one of reliving the abuse, and I won't survive anymore.

I am emotionally and physically tired right now writing this statement for 10 years. I have been fighting for my permanent protection here in Australia.

I do not have any means of livelihood to even start with in the Philippines, as my mental trauma will trigger me to break down and just be a useless woman, which was what my ex-husband has been saying to me for 24 years –that I was useless, misnomer and nothing – since there is no mental healthcare for me to afford my mental trauma care plan.

My ex-husband will punish me and file a case on me for publishing my memoir of all my abuse to him as he always does.

He will pay the police, courts and psychiatrists to say I was mentally crazy and unfit, then he will lock me up, which is my greatest fear.

I have been planning to write my memoir for more than four years now, but I could not finish it, as it was too painful until I had a lot of counselling and therapy.

Then I realised I should share it to humanity so that other women may learn from it, as what I experienced, with the rest of women, I did not know I was being abused. Therefore, reading the signs in my memoir will make them safe and attract a good, loving man.

This is my gift to myself and humanity. I do not mean to cause trouble on him, but knowing his abusive behaviour, he will have me kidnapped as soon as I arrive in the airport to say I have a case and am under arrest.

He has done a lot of fraud by paying offices, so he won't pay proper taxes with all our properties and he is used to bribing people around him. I do not want this kind of future harm on myself and my children.

My adult children will just side with their dad for their own protection, and they are bribed to lose their inheritance.

I do not have any help there, and the punishment of inhumane act of fabricating stories and locking me up in a mental facility is too significant harm.

I just thought I would rather die instead of being punished by him.

BEGGING THE GOD OF AUSTRALIA, HEAR MY PLEA

It was important to write my memoir as part of my recovery, and I was so inspired after reading Jess Hill's book, See What You Made Me Do.

I know and understand that this adds risk to my danger when I am sent back to the Philippines, hence my motivation for publishing in Australia is the best idea.

I only used this memoir for my own personal reasons, including my recovery and healing, and because I believe it is important for survivors to share their stories so other people feel supported to leave abuse.

I believe my past abuse, which I gave you a long history of abuse which has so much connection with the present – with Gileena being abused the same way I suffered. Therefore, the future harm is so much the same as what will happen to me and Arabella.

I believe that I don't have a future there anymore, as she knows her father will haunt me and abuse me further.

The future harm that I will face is a death sentence, as I don't have a home, life and motivation to live there anymore, as it reminds me of all the 24 years of abuse I suffered with him.

Even if someone gives me $1 million, I will not go back, as Australia is my home.

I feel so alive here and productive as a school teacher.

The real risk of harm to Arabella is also significant, as she will feel in limbo there without knowing anyone and the language barriers.

I know she loves her heritage, as she wants to learn the language from me, but it doesn't mean she wants to live there, as she does not want to be reminded of all the mental trauma she had, especially her fears before we left – that she will be taken away from me. That will happen when both of us will go back.

My fears for Arabella if she is returned to the Philippines

My ex-husband will try to take custody of Arabella when we return by paying a psychiatrist to say that I am mentally unfit. He will have full custody of my children.

Even if he did not make contact here in Australia to file custody,

I know for a fact that he does so many things to pry on me here, but he cannot buy Australia. If he takes Arabella, this time it would be more severe, as she has a long-standing mental trauma diagnosed of separation anxiety from me by a psychologist way back when she was 3 years old.

This will trigger, and as a mother I fear she won't survive.

Arabella will definitely suffer mentally, emotionally and socially if she is taken away from her friends and community here in Australia.

BEGGING THE GOD OF AUSTRALIA, HEAR MY PLEA

All her past mental trauma will surface again, and she will end up like Gileena – in and out of mental facility – and her father will further abuse her.

I believe that Arabella will struggle in school with the language and cultural barriers there, as Arabella is very independent, always likes to excel in school, has dreams of becoming a teacher and helping the teacher shortage.

All these dreams will be gone, and poor Arabella will have mental nervous breakdown.

How cruel if this would happen to Arabella when I tried hard to protect her here for 10 years.

Arabella will not get the same kind of mental healthcare here, just like the way STARTTS is doing for her.

She has counselling for her mental trauma once a month. Arabella can also access the school's mental well-being team and the school counsellor knows about her story, too, so the school looks after her.

Arabella shines at Camden High School – she was an emcee for their recognition day, had eight awards and one major award, and is a teacher helper in Physie dance club.

All these things will be gone as she will lose all the mental health care if she is sent back.

Arabella will not be able to access mental healthcare, as I do not have financial means to afford it, as it is too expensive.

There is no free mental healthcare in the Philippines.

It has very poor mental healthcare system. Also, the social stigma of having mental health issues is so strong in the Philippines.

Arabella will not survive that stigma.

She suffered enough while I was being abused by her father when she was in my womb.

It is time for Arabella to cut that continuing abuse in her life, and I will do everything as her mother to protect her.

Thus, I beg you to hear Arabella.

Why we cannot move to any other part of the country to be safe

Wherever I am, the mental trauma stays in my system now, so it doesn't matter whether I am relocated in the other parts of the Philippines or not.

I don't think the issue is relocation.

If it is, he and my mother-in-law will definitely haunt me and fabricate stories against me so I won't be able to claim my 50% conjugal properties, which I have the right for.

I would have to relive the same abuse I went through, as I found out that their grandmother is transferring properties titles under their names so I will be taken out from the title.

BEGGING THE GOD OF AUSTRALIA, HEAR MY PLEA

This is fraud and criminal Estafa case.

I have my evidence to file a case on my ex-husband and my mother-in-law, but I chose not to go to that path anymore.

I want my future to be just free from coercive control and manipulation of him.

We cannot get help from the police or local services to protect me and Arabella, as the graft and corruption there is so strong.

I mentioned the bribery cases in my previous statement.

My ex-husband is very good with bribing police, courts and any entities to ruin me and take Arabella from me.

Ruin means locking me up in a mental facility, which is a significant harm.

I had experienced him bribing our court in our annulment case.

I went there, and our annulment case was not moving, as the clerk said the judge retired. He told me not to go to court, as the lawyer he hired was so good.

I ended up still married to him there in the Philippines, but I filed for divorce here in Australia.

I heard about what happens to people trying to get help – they ended up missing in action. Azenith Briones, a veteran actress in the Philippines, was kidnapped by her two adult kids, as the neighbour saw them.

Two armed men dragged Azenith, with her two kids looking.

I read that they paid a mental facility for their mother to stay there, and the sons forced her to sign a deed of donation for their inheritance.

Being in a third world country, the lack of support in the Philippines is tantamount to a slave. When I was there after I left my abusive marriage,

I felt that I was in a dungeon of rations of food, as my kids controlled the household management in a six-bedroom house full of control and manipulation.

I do not have any support there to get free food, free school voucher, free mental healthcare, unlike here at Tahmoor Community Links where there are free food such as bread and any little staples that help a lot being a single mother.

I know a lot of people who just gave up and relocated to other parts of the world, as there is no future help and support from the government.

Some even have committed suicide out of despair.

Epilogue

What have I done for nearly 10 years, still struggling to be protected?

Have I been well for nearly 10 years?

Yes. I have been well. I am no longer attached to an abusive man.

I no longer throw the verbal abuse that my ex-husband ingrained to me.

With more than four years of counselling and still in counselling with STARTTS, I am able to work and function, as far as my triggers are concerned.

I no longer cry easily at work. I may still be sensitive, but I can verbalise it and face it with an objective mind. Sadly, I still suffer from PTSD. I still have nightmares and am hypervigilant that people might be paid to put trouble on me.

My fears are still with me. My devious, abusive past always haunts me. But I have so much help this time.

I have been helped by STARTTS, which was referred to me by the counsellor I had at Overcomers Outreach, Attachment and Addiction Specialist Penny Wilkinson. She advised me to give STARTTS a call about my plight. I am thankful to Amy, counsellor from STARTTS, that we had so much connection to be able to help me handle and manage my trauma and have my productive self-care.

My daughter and I are currently having a series of counselling, which helps us with our trauma, allowing us to feel safer and function in our daily lives with less anxiety.

Did I tie up the loose ends? I did.

I believe that through these pages, I have put across the message of breaking and cutting off the intergenerational trauma bonding between a mother to a daughter or to a son.

I believe I have imparted the life lessons not only to my family but to all who have enjoyed the feeling of healing and liberation in reading my book.

At present, we are called by the Administrative Appeals Tribunal with my daughter, and we'll have a hearing in January 2024. While my daughter Gilee is in the Philippines, crying out to be rescued here.

Last 7 November 2023, Gilee had a big argument with her dad about asking for money. She was able to record the abuse. Her

EPILOGUE

dad was accusing her of stealing money, when it was given to her by her godmother. Her dad grabbed the mobile phone when he saw that Gilee was recording it.

Gilee rang me on video call right after. She said she ran away with nothing, as her dad strangled, kicked, punched and pinched her. To be able to get back her phone, she kicked her dad in self-defence, then ran away. She was ringing me while it was happening, but I was in class. I had to go home in my Audrey Hepburn costume with a Fascinator crown, as it was Melbourne Cup that day. The principal was kind enough to give me a mental health well-being leave to check on my daughter. He is such a compassionate principal.

I do hope that Gilee can get a visa and be here in Australia one day to be able to cut the intergenerational trauma patterns of abuse of control.

"You're beautiful, but no one likes you and marry you!" my ex-husband once told me. Am I beautiful, but still no one loved me or wanted to marry me?

I am indeed beautiful, yes. I know, in my heart of hearts, that someone would love me and want to be with me for life. I know one day it will happen.

I believe in destiny. I believe what is meant to be will cross paths one day. One day, one lovely Australian man will marry me. One day, I will be protected permanently here in Australia with my daughter, Arabella.

In the meantime, this is my story. My beautiful story.

My undying love for my dear, beautiful daughter, Arabella, saved her from further abuse of being raised by her elder sisters instead of her dear mother.

My beautiful country, Australia, whom I chose to marry, loved me, liked me and looked after me.

Yes, I have cut the intergenerational trauma that was about to happen to Arabella. Yes, I got back the teaching job I lost from the years of marital distress and abuse I had suffered from my narcissistic ex-husband.

I was able to heal through the inspiration of my true blue Australian friends from church, my lovely friends and my supervisors.

The Principal, Deputy Principal, head teachers and staff are all supportive and very caring. I call this mateship – help is on the way.

I am now an esteemed NSW secondary teacher at a local high school.

"You're my favourite teacher, Ms Petersen." Not a day would pass that no student would say that to me.

"So, $a+a+a = 3a$? Is that how easy algebra is, Miss? You explained it so well!" a Year 7 remarked just recently while I was finishing this book's last chapter. It's proof that I got back all my skills and passion for teaching.

EPILOGUE

I almost lost it. I thought I had lost it before, as it took me a while to get back to the current version of myself. I have suffered from mental block and forgetfulness due to the years of blocking the verbal abuse that was said to me by my narcissistic ex-husband for 24 years.

But my mind is sharper now. Australia indeed resurrected me! Australia gave me my second lease of life! Australia cared for and loved me. Australia valued me.

Now I am proud to say that I contribute to the betterment of Australia's economy by being a teacher. I change people's lives and make a difference through my passion for teaching and building rapport with my students.

Thank you to all the lovely true blue Australians who have helped me along the way – my good friends, my lovely students.

A special mention to those who doubted me. Thanks a million for allowing me to show my inner soul to you. Thanks a million to one of my churchmates who said that it is not nice to have a cockatoo, as they are a nuisance when I mentioned that I'd love to have a cockatoo one day. I actually have a cockatoo now, and he is 4 years old. His name is Pedro. I love you, Pedro. He's my boy. He keeps me company. He is my true blue mate till my dying years; even after I am gone, cockatoos live more than 75 to 100 years.

I don't really listen to people who pretend they are helping me but are actually drilling a hole in the boat of life that I am rowing!

My Pedro would check on me if I wake up late as it is school holidays.

One time, he walked into my bedroom, as it was already 11 am. Every morning he would wake us up, as he knows I would go to work and Arabella would go to school. He is never a nuisance to me. Although a few times he does bite me, it's not that strong; just a cheeky bite, as I have been busy feeding him on my palm lately. Well, with this book I am writing after work, I pretty much devote myself with this.

He is my true blue Australian cockatoo mate that represents my love for Australia, my beloved, beautiful God's Country.

Thanks a million to those who tested my boundaries, allowing me to show my resilience.

Thanks a million to those who never committed; I know the best is yet to come.

"So, you want to write a book? You have money for it?" said a woman from the local writer's club I used to join. I took her word as a challenge instead of wallowing in the fact that I did not have the money. Yes, I have my esteemed teaching salary to publish my book, but not a million dollars.

Thanks a million to my employer who believed I could deliver.

EPILOGUE

I may have lost my share in the properties settlement in my marriage, but I gained infinite joy and happiness in being free from abuse as I see Arabella growing beautifully here in Australia.

She is in leadership council in high school. She is a teacher helper in Physie. She also loves dancing (I wonder where she gets it from).

She got chosen for Western Sydney University's Fast Forward Year 9 program.

Indeed, I made Arabella's place a better world to live in! I am so delighted to see Arabella love her high school life at Camden High School, as the principal, deputy principals and head teachers are very supportive in developing her full potential.

Just in the recent 2023 Recognition Awards for Year 9, she was the Master of Ceremonies with one of her best mate Jemma in school.

She also received eight awards, including:

- two Citizenship Awards for serving during the Year 7 Orientation Day and for being in the student leadership council,
- Core Values Award for displaying respect towards the school, staff and peers and for commitment to learning and contributing to a safe learning environment,
- Academic Excellence Award, and
- two Extracurricular Representation Awards for representing the school in a positive manner when undertaking an extracurricular event in the NAIDOC Week Presentation.

SAVING ARABELLA

On top of all these, Arabella dances at the local dance school. She is dancing ballet, contemporary, acro cheer, jazz, hip-hop and lyrical dance classes.

Pretty much, all my budget goes for her.

"Point well, Bea, Pointe Shoes (how dear) for Arabella!" (passing Pointe ballet assessment)

I dotingly posted on facebook and reels to the tune of classical ballet song.

This 2024, Arabella was approved to do Pointe Ballet class of which she was so excited. She will also do Ballet, Contemporary, Pre-Pointe Class and Lyrical for this years 2024 dance enrolment. Thank God she agreed to four dances this year, as she will start working on weekends already at a local takeaway shop.

She has been with Douglas Park Physie since she was 8 years old, and her teacher, Ms Melissa, treated her like her own daughter. Ms Emily and Ms Katie was also her Physie teachers.

Arabella has come a long way from her Physie, as she took centre stage in the grand finals for the first time in the Seniors team and got sixth place out of the 30 girls from the semi-finals.

EPILOGUE

She has developed her balance, flexibility and discipline over the six years she has been doing Physie.

I thank her teachers for being a great partner with me in parenting Arabella as a single mother.

Arabella indeed made this place a better world for herself by creating balance throughout her teenage life in and out of school activities. She also started reading the bible with me at Wilton Anglican Church. She read very well and eloquently.

I am so proud of you, Bea! You are like me – you made your mother proud of her youngest daughter, just as I had made mine.

I also plan to join Physie at Picton classes next year, as it keeps me focused and concentrated and helps my brain to relax.

In the meantime, I sing and dance in the classroom as I entertain my students to listen, which they love as well.

"Finish your work, then we will have music, and I will sing and dance for you."

"Wow, really Miss?"

"I'm never not gonna dance again," I played some songs and danced my dancing queen moves.

The next time I came to class, my students requested, "Ms Petersen, dance and sing for us while we finish our work."

My fondest memories of teaching was when I taught students with disabilities. I taught their geography class, and I told the class that we will have music as our brain break. When I played "Fly Away", one student, Grace, stood up and did her dance moves.

"Print, print, print", another student of mine, a lovely boy named Mitchell, suddenly uttered as he showed me his 100% score in his Spanish Duolingo game.

EPILOGUE

"Ms Petersen, what's your accent? I love your accent", another verbose student asked when I had a casual day with the students at the Support Unit.

"If you like the job, I will give you the contract", the Head Teacher for Admin told me before I started teaching my lovely students with special needs.

"I actually like teaching them, James. I find it so nurturing and fulfilling."

"OK, I will give you the contract for the next school year."

How deeply nurtured my soul was that day. And every day I teach, I nurture my soul.

These are my typical conversations with my lovely high school students, so I still do my dancing moves, as I cannot afford to go and have dance classes

I made my place a better world to live in!

I made it!

To all women, I hope you all make it too – to be who you are, to express yourself and shine in your own way!

I hope you all wish for my dreams to come true – a dream of being permanently protected here in God's country! A dream to grow old with a lovely Australian man! A dream for peace in humanity!

Goodnight to you all. I have to rest. I will see you all in the morning to share more of my Dancing Queen moves.

Dance with life, and life will dance with you!

So, I still am a Dancing Queen. "I'm ah, a dancing queen!"

Full Moon Winter
By: Bren Petersen'2018

Bloody Moon, see it,
Freaking amazing, I was so excited to see the full moon the eve
where the Blood moon appears.
it came during
Winter time, where everyone wants
to snuggle and not go see the Full Moon.
Not me. I love winter, I love cold, and the
shivers it gives me through my bones,
makes me feel I am home.
I am home with my Mum…
The eve of the Blood moon which only appears
every 15-17 years, I suddenly felt strange.
"I feel strange, I feel I am in a new journey!"
I don't know why I said that at 11:30 pm.
I came home, seeing the full moon, so bright, so clear,
like a fluorescent light, beaming, shining bright!
I still feel the change, change is coming!
I slept and woke up at 4:20 am to see the blood moon,
Bad luck, the full moon was covered with fibres of clouds, shades
of cloudy patches, I didn't see the blood moon at all!
Nevertheless, I still have this strange feeling, of being reborn, renewed,
and felt whole again!
This is what full Moon Winter brought me, a feeling of rejuvenation, of hope,
of living fully alive again!

I am back alive, after my hibernation!

Acknowledgements

To all my friends from the Philippines. Thank you to all my friends, lawyers, psychotherapists, psychiatrists. To my former teacher friends – Yoy, Simon, Divine, Mags – and the rest of my St Scho Manila colleague elementary (primary) teachers friends, Concha, Jenny and Didi, Simonette, Tina, Kat – my former student who is like a daughter to me – and Bing and Carmen for the realisation, enlightenment and moral support you gave me when I was struggling from my domestic violence abuse.

To all my Wollondilly local friends – Christina, Councillor Michael Banasik, Pam, Sandy Fleming, Councillor Susy Brandstater, Ben and Kate Boardman, Emma and Ruth Chafer of Wilton Anglican Church and, most specially, my Ingham's Supervisor, Kaylene Wood, for my work reference when I applied for my first teaching job at Wollondilly Anglican College.

To Marea, my good mate, I will always be your best mate who will look after you.

To Sam and Jay Sadek of Sadek Motor Group Camden NSW, thank you for always going way beyond to give my wish of a posh and nice elegant car, as cars are special to me and it's like my second house that should have all safety features.

To Glorya – yes, I'll never be poor again (your famous tagline). I have made that my mantra, hence I have achieved my goal to be back to teaching.

My colleagues and friends from my workplace, thanks for the welcoming atmosphere. To Morgan, Olga, James McManus and my fellow science teachers, and Mr, Pudsey thank you for making the bird perch of my lovely cockatoo, Pedro.

To my sisters and brothers who have helped my mother raise me, I am grateful for all the things you did for me when I was a little girl. All I can say is that I thank you for helping our mother raise me and looking after me when I was a child. Only gratefulness and love to my five siblings is what I wish to share with you here. I wish that one day we can share the love and the care that our mother had shown all of us here in Australia. To all my siblings, I wish great things for you all.

Thank you to my six beautiful children who have kept me going and gave me enough courage to live and to survive in my 24 years of controlling and manipulative domestic violence abuse.

My special thanks goes to Arabella for modelling God's strength and resilience. Thank you for being so mature and knowing that this world is still a place for you to shine. As young as you are, I can see your high-level thinking of wisdom and instincts. I thank the beautiful country of Australia for being a partner with me in

ACKNOWLEDGEMENTS

raising you here. We are indeed lucky to be in a lucky country of Australia.

My special thanks to Gilee, for rising above of herself now and conquering herself! Know that Mum is so proud of her fourth daughter Gilee, I love you and see you soon here in Australia.

To Camden High School, thank you for being a great partner in educating my dear daughter, Arabella. She felt so welcomed and belonged to your school.

To all my lovely students whom I have taught in the Philippines and Australia, thank you for nurturing my soul, as teaching nurtures my soul. You always make me feel respected, loved and cared for. I wish to let you know that my heart is big for you, and you all have a special spot in my heart. Indeed, you have made this place a better world to live in! How lovely to hear that my students loved to learn another language and would ask me to speak my native language. It showed how they're well-raised by their parents and that they are respectful and welcoming of other cultures.

Thank you to my school employer, my principal, Mr Luke Farthing, deputy principal and head teachers. I felt so belonged in your administration. Thank you for being a compassionate principal. I am honoured and humbled to be working with you. Thank you for the warm welcome you gave me as a multicultural teacher.

Kylie Captain, thank you for opening the Pandora's box. I have long dreamed of finishing and writing my book. Your books gave me an inspiration to finish mine. I admire your passion to make a difference and inspire people around you.

More Testimonials

"It is very interesting and powerful .

It depicts / shows the power and the greatest love of a Mother. Bren did struggle and did all in her power to protect and save her daughter from domestic violence .

All the best and good luck . You and Bea are always in my prayers."
**– Aunty Renee McFarlane,
kind and caring Filo-Australian Mate, Southern Highlands, NSW Australia**

I am delighted to know that Bren Petersen wrote a book about her journey to freedom. Her steadfast resolve to go to Australia with Arabellla was needed to start a new chapter in her life journey and to heal. Bren shows us her bravery, strength and resilience as well as her faith, hope and love filling her with miracles and blessings.

Remember Bren it is a process. I wish you the best in finding your worth and be the best version of yourself.

**– Concha Viri-Hontiveros,
(former Confidant/Counsel from the Philippines)**

To my beautiful Bren: - This book is all about strength and a child running to flee the mutilation of a marriage by violence inflicted by a callous man.

I am proud to be a part of this amazing woman's life.

There is a way out but a lot of strength will be needed.

**– Glynis King,
(Wilton/Picton Anglican Church bestmate**

"One in a Million"

**– Sandy Fleming, bestmate
Sandy's Van Owner Bren's favourite Meat Pie and Sausage Rolls**

Notes

NOTES

NOTES

SAVING ARABELLA

NOTES

www.ingramcontent.com/pod-product-compliance
Lightning Source LLC
Chambersburg PA
CBHW041317110526
44591CB00021B/2810